T0327685

AN ECONOMIC SPURT THAT FAILED

Dr. Ernest v. Koerber

An Economic Spurt That Failed

Four Lectures in Austrian History

BY ALEXANDER GERSCHENKRON

PRINCETON UNIVERSITY PRESS
PRINCETON, NEW JERSEY

Copyright © 1977 by Princeton University Press
Published by Princeton University Press, Princeton, New Jersey
In the United Kingdom: Princeton University Press, Guildford, Surrey

All Rights Reserved

Library of Congress Cataloging in Publication Data will
be found on the last printed page of this book

Publication of this book has been aided by the Whitney Darrow
Publication Reserve Fund of Princeton University Press

This book has been composed in VIP Times Roman

Printed in the United States of America
by Princeton University Press, Princeton, New Jersey

"Die Welt steht auf kein' Fall mehr lang"
> JOHANN NESTROY, *Lumpazzi-Vagabundus*, 3:8

"Egerunt, sed non peregerunt, suspiciendi tamen sunt"
> SENECA, *Epistles*, VII:64

Contents

Illustrations

Preface

THE TOPIC OF THIS BOOK has been with me for some fifteen years, running along, and competing with, other projects. I found it irresistibly attractive. For the undeservedly neglected episode that is the subject matter of this study is of general historical significance.

Many people will agree that the lack of internal cohesion of the Austrian-Hungarian Monarchy was one of the many causes of World War I, and, therefore, any attempt, however abortive it may have been, to increase that cohesion may rightly lay claim to general attention.

But there is an additional, more personal reason for my interest. In my studies of the industrial history of Europe, I have devoted much time and effort, blackening a good many pages in the process, to the phenomenon of discontinuous spurts as an integral part of industrialization in conditions of economic backwardness. I found that a peculiarity of those spurts was the appearance of what I termed "substitutions" for the "missing prerequisites." Use of banks and/or government budgets were viewed as examples of such substitutions. Yet a spurt of economic development engineered by government action represents something quite unusual in the history of *Western* countries. And this is precisely what the present study is all about. As does every empirical case with its specificities and individualities, so too the Austrian case enriches our general approach to, and our comprehension of, industrial history and, beyond it, of problems of economic development in which not just the economists but all social scientists maintain keen interest.

For these reasons, once the thought of examining the facts and problems involved in the Austrian case had occurred to me, the subject was never far from my mind. But it was the invitation to deliver, in April 1973, two Janeway Lectures at Princeton University that first prompted me to put on paper what was to become an extended outline for this study. It is, therefore, fitting indeed for the finished product to be published by Princeton University Press.

In the summer following the lectures I went to Vienna to work in the archive of the Austrian Ministry of Finance. The purpose was to find documentary evidence for statements that had been ventured in the oral presentation as speculations and conjectures. The trip proved successful beyond all expectations and yielded materials that have come to constitute the contents of Lecture Three of this book.

I must tender my thanks to the American Philosophical Society for a grant used to finance the journey to Vienna and my sojourn there. I must also express my sincere gratitude for the assistance I received from the staff of the *Finanzarchiv* (Hofrat Dr. Walter Winkelbauer, Herr Franz Zinner, and Frau Anna Schardinger), an assistance offered eagerly, gracefully, and most knowledgeably. It is, furthermore, a pleasure for me to thank the Chairman of the Department of Economics at Harvard University, Professor James S. Duesenberry, who despite great budgetary pressures very generously offered the services of a secretary to a retired member of his department. And, last but not least, I must mention Mrs. Elizabeth Miele, who typed and retyped the ever-changing manuscript with great efficiency and understanding and, what is even more, with unshakable good cheer.

A word on the form of the book. I feel that it is proper to have preserved the division in lectures (rather than chapters) because the two Janeway Lectures actually encompassed the whole of its contents, even though much research, archival and other, was done after those lectures. As a consequence the style of the presentation is not uniform. I have deliberately preserved the form of oral delivery in the first part of Lecture One. But, despite a famous example in literature, I felt that it would be artificial to press such a form (mostly in the use of personal pronouns) upon those portions of the study that in fact never were heard by an audience. Somewhat hybrid as the result is, it at least gives the reader an inkling of the style of the Janeway Lectures in which the book originated.

A.G.

AN ECONOMIC SPURT THAT FAILED

The Road Before, the Moment, and its Hero

THESE LECTURES will deal with a brief but significant episode in the history of Austria in the early years of the century. The episode is primarily concerned with economic development, and the attempt will be made to see it in the light of my general approach to the industrial development of Europe. The lectures, therefore, were planned as a study in the *economic* history of Austria. But economic, political, and social factors were so closely intertwined in the history of the country in general, and especially so during the short period under review, that it did not seem right to include the word "economic" in the subtitle. To increase my titular misgivings, the Kiplingesque title that I have chosen for this book raises some problems.

First of all, the title is probably unwise. Counsels of ancient wisdom tell us that a presentation should begin with a *captatio benevolentiae*. But failures rarely excite benevolence, and men's interest in them is easily suppressed. The listener's ear is eagerly lent to success stories and the reader's eye auspiciously turns in the same direction. The student of failure is likely to fail. The awkward title may cause my audience to melt away, if not flee in disorder; and very soon I may have to derive comfort from the equally ancient saying that walls also have ears. This contingency is much to be feared. For, as people say who like to use words that are much too big for their minds, though not for their mouths, our society or our culture disapproves of solitude, to say nothing of loneliness. If nevertheless, perversely and deviantly, I am willing to brave the opprobrium, the reason does not lie in any ambition to emulate Ibsen's Doctor Stockman. The point rather is that overriding the tactics of salesmanship there is the methodological problem of scholarship. The question was asked once: "Why should not Failure have its Plutarch as well as success?", and an eminent, and eminently successful, Victorian felt he could brush the question aside by explaining that "a record of failure would probably be found excessively depressing as well as uninstructive reading."[1] Depressing and uninstructive? I cannot hope that my story will elevate your spirits, although it might, were it told by a Plutarch. But for the rest I disagree strongly. I do believe that there is much to learn from some historical failures, and an economic spurt that failed may cast a ray of unfailing light upon things and events that should not be left in obscurity.

There are, of course, failures and failures. There are failures that are counterpoised by success. Napoleon's failure at Waterloo was Wellington's success. But there are also asymmetrical failures—cases of defeats without victories. A failure of this kind will occupy us in these lectures. These failures are the stepchildren of history. Their neglect may be understandable, but must remain unjustified until we have explored the causes of the failure and in addition perhaps have raised the problem of alternative outcomes, discussing, that is, not only why things happened as they did, but also what might have happened instead. I do not feel that I have to apologize for raising at this early point the specter of counterfactual history—that old bugaboo of historians who are anxious to prevent people from asking pertinent and interesting questions and have neither the wit nor the imagination for asking those questions themselves. As Cournot once said, the function of predictions is not to foretell the future, but to cast light on the present.[2] This, properly understood, is precisely the function of "might-have-beens" in history. Whether avowedly or not, they are involved in any discussion of "errors" committed and are, therefore, especially, relevant in cases of "purposes mistook," which in our minds are associated with failures.

The Shakespearean phrase, however, must not blind us to the complexity of the concept of failure in varying historical situations. The disparity between aims and attainments may be no more than one aspect of the phenomenon. Even within that aspect there may be the problem of measuring the disparity and of determining the degree of failure, a task possibly compounded by

[1] Samuel Smiles, *Self-Help*, London, 1958, p. 34.
[2] A. Cournot, *Souvenirs, 1760-1860*, Paris, 1913, p. 251.

4

the fact that a multiplicity of aims may be connected with a given complex of action, involving also varying degrees of attainments. And beyond that lies the troublesome question: "whose aims and what aims?" The aims of the authors, of the initiators and pursuers of the action? The aims openly announced or the aims secretly entertained, which may well have differed from the former? Then there are the contemporaries and the aims the contemporaries, rightly or wrongly, imputed to the action, possibly attaching different coefficients of importance to the individual aims and as likely as not disagreeing among themselves on the aims as well as on the attainments, and accordingly also on the degree of failure and possibly on the very fact of failure that may be indubitable to some and questionable to others. Finally, the same problems confront the historian. He must scrutinize the yardsticks used in the past. But he must do more. He must cut and calibrate his own yardsticks, taking into account effects of actions and potentialities of effects that may have remained unperceived by the contemporaries whose views, biases, and evaluations inevitably enter the complex of the historian's *explicanda* and will be some of the signposts leading him to his final judgment.

To be sure, there are unambiguous and uncomplex failures. We know what Napoleon wanted to achieve at Waterloo, and no one disagrees in appraising the result. This is not to deny that the historiography of battles has its problems (who won at Jutland?) and that at times even the loser at a chess game may feel that he has achieved a "moral" victory. But on the whole, the preceding cogitations are irrelevant in the context of "symmetrical" failures. By contrast, they apply with considerable force to the much more complex situation of an engineered spurt of economic development, a spurt that was designed not only to solve important economic problems but also to cure many grave ills of the body politic. Such an episode is the subject matter of these lectures. It occupied a little bit less than a full quinquennium, lasting from early 1900 through 1904.

It is fortunate that in this case at least, the points of inception and termination of the episode are clearly marked by the appointment and resignation of a prime minister, Ernest von Koerber. Although not without assistance, Koerber was the architect of policies that filled the lustrum, and we will refer henceforth to the period and to the policies pursued as the "Koerber era" or the "Koerber experiment." Nevertheless, however sharp the chronological demarcations, cutting into the seamless web at any given moment is never easy. The operation requires some knowledge and understanding of the immediate antecedents. Hence a number of prefatory observations is indispensable before I can proceed to selection, description, and interpretation of events that were encompassed in the Koerber era.

One way both to start the story and to intimate the problems and the difficulties of the moment and of the past is to say that on January 18, 1900, the Crown, that is, Emperor Francis Joseph, appointed Koerber as the Prime Minister (*Ministerpraesident*) of Austria. This innocuous statement is curiously inexact as far as its last term is concerned. The prime minister of Austria? But strictly, that is to say, officially speaking, there was no country by that name at that time. The name *Austria* appeared only in international relations in the compounds "Austria-Hungary" or "Austrian-Hungarian Monarchy." But the western "half" (*Reichshaelfte*) of the Dual Monarchy—the Austria of the colloquial speech—went under the unbelievably cumbersome participial mouthful of "The Kingdoms and Lands Represented in the Parliament."[3] At the same time also another name, much less strenuous on tongue and pen but thoroughly inappropriate geographically, was in wide literary usage: Cisleithania. The name referred to the river Leitha, a minor tributary of the Danube, which for a brief stretch separated the province of Lower Austria from that of West-Hungary (now, except for the town of Oedenburg, a part of the Republic of Austria under the name of Burgenland). A traveler between the two capitals, Vienna and Budapest, had indeed to cross the river, but large parts of the Western "half," such as Galicia and Bucovina, were if anything far east of

---

[3] *Die im Reichrat vertretenen Koenigreiche und Laender.* It was much later, more than a decade after the end of the period with which we are here concerned, in the years preceding the final collapse of the Monarchy that an Imperial decree at length gave "Austria" an official standing.

6

the Leitha, while the location of others, such as Bohemia and Moravia, had no visible relation to the river.

These nominal oddities and embarrassments are more than historical curiosities. For they are symptomatic of the far less than perfect unity and cohesion of the political entity over which Ernest von Koerber was called upon to govern—a state or half-of-a-state, populated by Germans, Czechs, Poles, Ruthenians, Croatians, Slovenians, and Italians, none of whom nursed feelings of affection for the others. And on the other side of the river Leitha, in Transleithania, the Hungarian government under a Hungarian prime minister lorded it over disaffected Slovaks, Croatians, Serbians, and Rumanians and at the same time continued to bargain hard with the "Austrian" government, eagerly trying to enhance the position of the Hungarian "half" and in the process jeopardizing the unity and cohesion of the whole Monarchy, a problem quite apart from that of the internal predicaments of the two "halves."

The difficulties of the whole and of the parts have a long history, but they—and particularly those of the "Austrian" half— had acquired especial gravity by the time of Koerber's elevation to the presidency of the cabinet. The appropriate starting point for a brief summary may well be the defeat Austria—then still unambiguously Austria—suffered at the hands of Prussia in 1866.

Military victory and defeats played a determining role in Austrian political life since the accession to the throne of Francis Joseph. After the revolution of 1848, the victory over the Austrian people and the Hungarians (by Russian proxy) as well as the discomfiture of Sardinia—the solitary military achievement of the reign in foreign wars—had inaugurated the long years of absolutist rule. Austria's defeat by France and Piedmont in 1859 led to the first adoption of limited constitutional measures. But the disaster of 1866 had more far-reaching consequences. Victor Adler, paraphrasing Custine's celebrated adage, once coined the description of Austrian political system as *"Absolutismus gemaessigt durch Schlamperei."* Absolutism tempered by what? The not quite literary *Schlamperei* is so specifically and relevantly Austrian as to defy unambiguous translation. "Muddle," "sloppiness," "mess"—none of these will quite do, although all of them in conjunction might. Holofernes in Nestroy's delightful travesty says: "Take the corpses away. I can't stand any *Schlamperei*." At any rate, "absolutism reformed by defeats" would be a formula, much less witty than Adler's crisp epigram, but quite as correct historically. The defeat at Koeniggraetz profoundly changed the political structure of the state. It created in undue haste the Dual Monarchy and brought the December constitution of 1867.

The Dual Monarchy—the regime's reconciliation with Hungary—involved establishment of two states within Austria-Hungary with two cabinets and two parliaments in each of the "halves," with the whole somewhat tenuously tied together by the Crown, a common army, and a common foreign policy, with a third cabinet consisting of a common minister of foreign affairs, a common minister of war, and a common minister of finance, the last two having their replicas within the cabinets of the "halves." In addition, a third parliament-like body (*Delegationen*) with representations of the two parliaments was introduced. The economic, financial, and monetary policies were not predetermined as common once and for all, but had to be settled every ten years by a compromise settlement between the two cabinets and parliaments (*Ausgleich*). The geographic and political boundaries separating the halves were essentially determined by the romantic reference to the "historical" rights of the Crown of Saint Stephen, which most importantly meant that Croatia and Slavonia (despite some hesitations and broken pledges) were to be included in the Hungarian half. The Croatian peasants, a limited autonomy of Croatia notwithstanding, came to be ruled by the Hungarian gentry. The reconciliation with Hungary at the expense of the South Slavs was a fateful and fatal decision as became fully obvious a half-century later. But by limiting the Austrian governments' freedom (and radius) of action, the decision also had a certain bearing on the specific problems to be discussed in these lectures. Dalmatia, also mostly populated by Croatians, remained with the Austrian half, but somewhat uncertainly so, and continued as an object of Hungarian claims. The complex arrangement, ill-thought through, created more problems than it solved, and particularly so for the internal structure of Cisleithania.

The constitution of 1867 included a modern bill of rights that,

8

however, did not prevent laws regarding the freedom of press, association, and assembly from being administered in an authoritarian and at times rudely high-handed fashion. Even when no "state of emergency" (*Ausnahmszustand*) or martial law (*Standrecht*) were proclaimed, as was to happen several times, newspapers were subject to severe restrictions and could be and were confiscated without recourse to courts (*objektives Verfahren*), and the bureaucracy felt free to prohibit or dissolve meetings. The Parliament (*Reichsrat*), that is, its lower chamber, the *Abgeordnetenhaus*, was elected first indirectly by the provincial diets and then directly, but on the basis of a highly restricted and unequal suffrage, the relatively very small electorate being grouped in four classes (large landed estates, chambers of commerce, towns, and country communes); the masses of urban inhabitants and especially industrial labor were deprived of any franchise. Thus the system was burdened with the thorny problem of the gradual widening of suffrage until the final introduction of general franchise of 1907—a specifically social problem and, as such, supplemental to the problem of discord among the nationalities. Legislation was reserved to the Parliament, with the sanction of laws by the Crown, except that the latter, in specified circumstances, could legislate on the basis of the emergency article 14 of the constitution. The government, appointed by the Crown, was responsible to the Parliament but in fact served at the pleasure of the Monarch. Moreover, time and again, cabinets managed to survive defeats in the parliament. Thus, the constitutionalism of the system, too, was well-tempered by the strong position of the Emperor and the strength of bureaucracy, as well as by the general atmosphere and tradition of the authoritarianism—the *Obrigkeitsstaat*. The use and abuse of article 14 and the arbitrary actions of bureaucracy were strong elements of absolutism and police state that were rife beneath the constitutional veneer.

Erected in a hurry by inept architects, the duplex house, or rather the duplex tenement, of the Dual Monarchy began to reveal manifold structural inadequacies almost as soon as the building was completed. In particular, the house rules of the December constitutional acts proved ill suited to assure peaceful relations between the landlord and the tenants as well as among the tenants themselves. Despite the existence of the provincial diets, whose laws, too, required imperial sanction, the constitution envisaged a centralist state. In administration, the cabinet in Vienna with the support of the Crown was to be the landlord. But the cabinet was in some sense responsible to the parliament, and the latter was therefore to exercise landlord function not only in legislation. But who was supposed to be the landlord there? In Hungary, the Hungarians lorded it over the non-Hungarian nationalities. The symmetrical structure of the Dual Monarchy presupposed that the same functions were to be fulfilled by the Germans. German majorities were to make the laws, German bureaucracy was to administer and German judges to apply them. The German language in practice, though not in law, would be the state language (*Staatssprache*).

But here lay crucial problems. Czech statehood and Czech nationhood had perished in the storms of the counterreformation.[4] The hiatus in national consciousness lasted for about two centuries before the revival. Presumably, its advent was connected with the economic changes brought about by the nineteenth century. The nascent Czech bourgeoisie and the Czech intelligentsia became the original carriers of a movement of national aspiration that was to penetrate far down into the Czech population. The compact with Hungary produced a deep shock in the Czech lands. What was good for the Hungarians should have been also good for the Czechs. If the Hungarians referred to the lands under Saint Stephen's crown, the Czechs, too, had their own romantic historical memories and their own reference to the lands under the Saint Wenzel's crown (the Bohemian *Staatsrecht*). The dualism of the 1867 arrangement should have been, it was felt, supplemented and supplanted by a "trialist" arrangement. Trialism, to be created by detaching the South Slavic lands from Hungary, later became the subject of vague plans that never even began to ap-

[4] The Czech claim that it was only the policy of Maria Theresa in the middle of the eighteenth century that gave the *coup de grâce* to Czech statehood is of little relevance in my context. See Karel Kramář, *Anmerkungen zur boehmischen Politik*, Aus dem Boehmischen uebersetzt von Josef Penížek, Vienna, 1906, pp. 74, 132; and Karl Kramář, *Das boehmische Staatsrecht*, Vienna, 1896, pp. 14-22.

proach fruition. But trialism achieved by the transformation of the Czech provinces into a third political entity beside Hungary and the rest of Cisleithania for one brief moment seemed to become much more than a vague plan, only to be abandoned when the moment had passed.

Nevertheless, the Czech aspirations could not be ignored. Throughout most of the decade of the seventies the Germans dominated the Reichsrat. It may be left open whether sociologically speaking their rule could be described as that of the large German bourgeoisie, as has been fairly persuasively claimed. But politically it certainly was the heyday of Austrian liberalism, removing the legacies of the absolutist period, above all, the concordat with Rome and beyond that modernizing the structure of Cisleithania in a variety of ways. Even more importantly, the German rule was centralist, stressing the unity of the Monarchy. The centrifugal, "federalist" as they were called, tendencies came from many parts. The Italian *irridenta* in South Tyrol was active and at times very visible. Even the "history-less" (*geschichtslose*) Slovenians in southern Styria and Carniola awoke to raise a strong voice against the Germans both in Vienna and in Graz, the capital of Styria. The Ruthenians fought against the supremacy of the Poles in Galicia. But all those drives paled into relative insignificance compared with the Czech national protest. The latter, ever-present and ever-rising, had quickly become the focus of internal politics. Three times between the compact of 1867 and the inception of Koerber's ministry major attempts were made to solve the vexed problem.

The first attempt occurred in 1871 under the ministry of Count Hohenwart. An Imperial rescript referred to the traditional rights of the Bohemian Crown and promised the formal recognition of those rights in a solemn coronation ceremony of the Emperor as the King of Bohemia that was envisaged for an unspecified future. Simultaneously, the government submitted to the Bohemian diet a bill stipulating far-reaching equality of Germans and Czechs in Bohemia in every respect, including the parity of the two languages, and projecting a reorganization of the Diet by division into two national groups with qualified veto rights so as to safeguard each nation against discriminatory bills. Finally, the

11

so-called "Fundamental Articles," agreed upon with the Czechs and also presented to the Diet, would have greatly expanded the legislative rights of the Diet at the expense of the Reichsrat in Vienna. (The plan even included a common diet for the three lands of Saint Wenzel's crown.) This was the extreme of "federalism" and came close to a trialist solution. But German resistance in Vienna and dissension even within the cabinet (in conjunction with Hungarian objections) led within a few weeks to Hohenwart's downfall. The defeat of the "federalist" forces was complete, and the attempt remained an episode.

Unlike later events in the last years of the century, the disappointment of the Czechs, great as it was, did not produce dramatic effects. The Bohemian Czechs continued their policy of boycotting the Reichsrat almost to the end of the seventies. But the problem remained. In 1879, Count Taaffe became Prime Minister and remained in office for fourteen long years. Under him the German predominance was broken. Taaffe's rule—the right-wing cabinet—was based on what was called the "Iron Ring," a curious coalition composed of Slavs (the Czechs and the Poles), the clerical forces, and the "feudals," that is to say, mainly owners of large estates in Bohemia who essentially were "federalist." Under their leadership, the Czechs at length appeared in the Reichstag. The curiosity lay in the fact that the "feudals" belonged to the mostly German high aristocracy. Their willingness to favor and to promote the Czech aspirations may indicate that they were primarily moved by their antagonism to the German bourgeoisie. The antagonism may have been directed against the liberal policies of the latter, but it may also have derived from the conflict of economic interests. To the extent that the latter supposition is true, it suggests that economic interests may have had a priority over, and may have been stronger than, national interests. This contingency is something that must be kept in mind as relevant in a much broader sense to the appraisal of policies we will consider. The problem of the relative weight of economic and national interests will indeed be crucial in this respect.

In principle, the years of the Taaffe administration were good for the Czechs. In 1880, an edict of the minister of justice stipulated that in Bohemia and Moravia the resolutions of the authorities, be they oral or written, were to be issued in the language originally used by the plaintiff or petitioner. In fact, even in the case of official documents, emitted upon the initiative of the authority, the language used was to be the language of the person to whom the document was addressed. The edict, therefore, stipulated the parity of the Czech language as an "external" language, i.e. the language used in the relations between the authorities and the population. And the concept of "authorities" was comprehensive indeed, embracing as it did administration, courts, and the offices of state prosecutors. This was a step of considerable significance. Much more was involved than a matter of national pride. The question of language was a decisive question of power. Predominance of the German language meant German predominance in the administration. At stake was no less than the national composition of administrative and judicial services. In fact, linguistic "parity" meant more than establishing the administrative parity. For the Germans appeared unable or at least unwilling to learn Czech, while German, having been the *lingua franca* of the regions, was more or less known to most of the Czechs aspiring to positions in the bureaucracy. As a result, considerable numbers of Czechs entered the ranks of the civil service and of the courts in Bohemia and Moravia, including the large areas, particularly of the former province, where the population was overwhelmingly German. The German element was being pushed back. Left open by the language decree was the question of the "internal" language, i.e. the language of the internal transactions of the authorities. Later on, the problem was to assume a central significance. For the time being, other concessions followed. The whole lower educational structure received strong injections of Czech schools. Czech institutions of higher learning were established. For a while it seemed as though the Czech problem was on the road to solution, but appearances were deceptive.

The measures of the government and the reduced position of the Germans in the Reichstag produced vehement opposition among the Germans. Extremist, violently anti-Czech, political groupings arose among the Austrian Germans, which, more and more, were directed against the Monarchy by raising the specter of the *Anschluss* to the German Empire at least of the German-

13

populated provinces (including the Sudeten in the North). The vehement German reaction could not fail to produce a Czech reaction in the form of considerable radicalization in the Czech nationalist camp, which was reinforced by the more or less natural downward spreading of Czech nationalism along the layers of social structure. After a decade of the Taaffe rule, the 1889 elections brought the victory of the radical "Young-Czechs" who unlike their predecessors, the "old-Czechs," were unwilling to tolerate any longer the leadership of the local German aristocracy or the leadership of the clericals who had strenuously fought for the abridgment of public elementary education and its subjection to the *ecclesia militans*, a problem that for the Czechs was even more important than for the Germans. Altogether, the Young-Czechs protested vigorously against what they called the crumb (*Brosamen*) policy of the Austrian government, something that today, even less elegantly, would be called "tokenism."

From 1889 on the Taaffe regime was in decline. In the following year the government tried to solve the Czech question through a compact between the Germans and the Czechs. Among other things, the school administration and supervision were to be split along national lines. The same was envisaged for the future with regard to courts by national delimitation of court districts. It was symptomatic of the changes that had taken place that the projected compromise included at least as many concessions to the Germans as to the Czechs, and it was the radical Czechs in the Bohemian Diet who, in protest, engineered turmoil and turbulence in the Diet (1893). This was obstruction, physical obstruction, a harbinger of things to come—and not in a provincial diet, but in the Parliament itself. The disorders in the Diet spread to the streets and led to the proclamation of the "emergency state" (*Ausnahmszustand*) over Prague, which was to last for some 25 months, to arrests and trials.

Taaffe, pressed from all sides, tried as the last recourse a reform of parliamentary suffrage that would have introduced general franchise into the classes of towns and country municipalities (Landgemeinden), though without abandoning the electoral class system at all. The political labor movement, the Social Democrats, had greatly increased their strength since the days when

14

the Taaffe government had held the movement down with "emergency states." But the Social Democratic leadership did not consider the time right for an all-out struggle for the electoral reform. That was to come years later. Both the aristocrats and the German Liberals in the Reichsrat objected vehemently to an extension of franchise that, the Liberals claimed, was bound to lead to a downfall of the German bourgeoisie. Thus Taaffe succeeded in solving neither the problem of the electoral reform, which was to become the most pressing problem of social policy, nor the problem of Czech nationalism. His failure with regard to the latter set the stage for the third attempt at a settlement that, too, proved a failure, but in its turn set the stage for the highly critical situation in which Koerber found the country upon his assumption of office. About this attempt a few words must be said in concluding this preliminary description.

To the extent that Count Taaffe lives in history, he is remembered as a man of a low time-horizon. He himself once described his policies as "muddling through," which is an inadequate rendition of *Fortwursteln*, the earthy Viennese term that came easily from the lips of that jovial and lighthearted Austrian aristocrat of Irish descent.[5] The word may have fitted Taaffe's reliance upon the policy and bureaucratic machinery of repression in a way that was perhaps lighthearted, but heavyhanded and not at all jovial. Still, Taaffe had at least tried to find some solution to the twin problems of nationalism and electoral reform. The stubborn and narrow-minded rejection of electoral reform by the privileged interests in the Parliament was an even more impressive testimony for the inability to see beyond the given moment than ever had been supplied by the master of the "muddling through" strategy. In any event, when the Taaffe government fell, leaving the country with several untreated and slowly festering ulcers, few, if any, had a time-horizon high enough to foresee, let alone foretell, the political predicament that befell the land after a surprisingly short period.

[5] I can safely disregard a recent assertion by Hugo Hantsch (based on an unpublished dissertation) according to which Taaffe was not himself the originator of the term. Hugo Hantsch, *Die Geschichte Oesterreichs*, Vienna, 1955, Vol. II, p. 598.

One: The Road Before, . . .

Almost exactly four years after Taaffe's demise in the late fall of 1897, Vienna received the visit of a very distinguished foreigner. Mark Twain came, established himself in the visitors' gallery of the lower chamber of the parliament (*Abgeordnetenhaus*), and watched the proceedings with a sharp eye and amused irony, well mingled with astonishment and disgust. He set down his observations and impressions in a report he called "Stirring Times in Austria." What he had seen was stirring indeed. It was, Mark Twain believed, something "history will be talking of five centuries hence" and "the memory of which will outlast all the thrones that exist today."[6] The thrones the great writer of a great Republic must have been thinking of when he penned those lines have long disappeared. In the course of the three-quarters of a century that separates us from the events Mark Twain bore witness to, world history—a highly unpleasant world history—has supplied us with *memorabilia* of a quite different order. Even in the narrow field of parliamentary history, in the little republic that had emerged from the ruins of the Dual Monarchy a freely elected parliament was altogether suppressed by the ruthless fiat of a dictatorial mediocrity. Yet against the background of the declining decades of the nineteenth century the goings on in the pseudo-classical building on the *Ringstrasse* in Vienna were arresting, to say the least.

As Mark Twain looked down over the railing of the gallery into the huge semicircular pit of the chamber, he saw a picture of lunatic frenzy. Many deputies, armed with the removable boards of their desks (Twain, the well-trained reporter, provided exact measurements of the boards), created an infernal noise by hitting the tops of the desks with the boards. The coarsest Viennese wit and the darkest recesses of the Vienna dialect were mobilized for words of unprintable abuse the deputies hurled at each other at the top of their voices (acute as were Mark Twain's powers of observation, he missed the interesting anthropological fact that German curses were anal and Slavic curses genital). In the midst of the cacophony, a man stood behind the tribune making his speech. Undisturbed by the wild scenes around and below him, he spoke

---

[6] Mark Twain, *How To Tell a Story*, Hartford, Connecticut, 1900, p. 248.

and spoke at length—in fact, for a total of twelve (according to some sources—thirteen) hours, sticking throughout to his subject, which happened to be the highly technical problem of the compact with Hungary. The record performance elevated the speaker to the position of a hero. The desk hitters, the shouters, and the abusers were engaged in what was known as physical obstruction, but the heroic speaker was practicing one of the forms—and there were many—of technical obstruction. Physical or technical, the purpose of the twin strategies was one and the same—to paralyze the parliament by making the conduct of its business impossible. A few days later, with Mark Twain continuing his untiring and fascinated watch, the climax came. The president of the house (a member from Galicia) flagrantly broke the order of business by claiming false recourse to a vote that had never taken place or at least remained entirely unnoticed. At the next meeting he was hustled out by a group of deputies who had stormed his tribune, and thereupon Clio entered the sacred hall in the guise of sixty helmeted policemen who physically removed the obstreperous deputies from the chamber. The unheard-of deed was done. The talented reporter on the gallery had a magnificent conclusion for his magnificent copy.

What was the background of these events, whose impact remained to plague the Danubian Monarchy for the remaining years of its existence? Some interludes followed Taaffe's resignation, but then Count Badeni (October 1895) became the head of the government. A Pole of Italian descent, Badeni had been the governor of Galicia and had ruled the province with an iron hand, ruthlessly suppressing the Ruthenian as well as, for that matter, the Polish peasants in West Galicia. The strong man, unused to effective opposition in his home province, felt he could cut the Gordian knots of the Monarchy with a few sharp strokes. He went to work briskly. In 1896 he managed to get through the parliament an electoral reform that without abolishing the class system added to the four classes a "general class" (*allgemeine Kurie*) in which the franchise was general and which received assigned 72 seats in the chamber (as against the 85 seats assigned to the class of large, landed estates). The reform was limited indeed, but it provided an opportunity for the first time for a small number of representatives of the labor movement to enter the parliament.

Encouraged by this success, Badeni went on to attempt "solving" the Czech problem. In April 1897, he issued the celebrated decrees for Bohemia and Moravia according to which the authorities were ordered to use the language in which they had been addressed in *all* transactions concerning the respective cases. The decree thus established the Czech language as the "internal" language. In addition, knowledge of both languages was made obligatory for all the civil servants in the two provinces. These decrees provoked the fury of the Germans. They objected violently to Badeni's method of using the instrument of decrees rather than that of a law for the purpose. They objected even more violently to the substance of the decrees, which failed to provide any special treatment for the large segments of the provinces that were overwhelmingly German.

Parity of the two languages was, of course, bound to cause hardships, which were reinforced by the pattern of national settlement in Bohemia. It was difficult for a German defendant of a civil suit brought in Czech language by a Czech plaintiff to study the court documents and to follow the trial that had to be conducted in Czech. The Germans never tired of making this point. They were less eager to admit that for long years Czechs—and particularly uneducated Czech peasants (though not the educated Czechs)—had been victims of the same hardships. Here the crux of the matter was again power. The decrees, the Germans felt, implied surrendering the German population to the rule of Czech bureaucrats. The Germans believed the decrees would change the German character of the close German-settled districts in the North and South of Bohemia. They advocated division of the province into a German and a Czech Bohemia. The pattern of settlement in Bohemia (unlike the situation in Moravia) would have made such a separation possible. But such a measure was not acceptable at all to the Czechs, because it would destroy the historical unity of the "lands of Saint Wenzel's Crown." For the rest, neither hardships and inconveniences nor the balance of bureaucratic and judicial power suffices to explain the acerbity of the emotions aroused. There is little doubt that, apart from all practical considerations, language was an abstract value in itself, more or less vaguely connected with the idea of national culture and its defense. It was perhaps paradoxical that barbarous means came to be employed in defense of culture and that in the process the political culture of the country was threatened with destruction. At any rate, for reasons, good and bad, rational and irrational, equitable and inequitable, the Badeni decrees were received and understood by the Germans as a violent blow directed against the German nationality in Austria. Since the Germans in the parliament could muster no majority against the decrees, they took recourse to filibuster—the mighty and fateful weapon of parliamentary obstruction. That was the background of the disgraceful scenes which disheartened Mark Twain.

Parliamentary obstruction is a two-edged sword, or rather a curious combination of a rapier and a bludgeon. On the one hand, it is an exquisitely legalistic tool. Parliamentarism implies rule by majority, but "majority" by definition presupposes the existence of minority and the process of majority formation is inconceivable without full protection of the rights of minority. Hence the meticulous provisions of the order of business, and hence the manifold opportunities to delay and to impede the conduct of proceedings by strictest possible adherence to those provisions. This became known as the technical obstruction, and, even though it did not originate in Austria, it was in Vienna that technical obstruction developed into both a fine art and a persistent phenomenon. As parliamentarism rolled on through the nineteenth century, spreading, recovering from setbacks, and apparently designed to become the dominant form of government, obstruction suddenly threatened to stem the advance. A fatal flaw appeared in the mighty engine of progress, and men began to speak of the crisis of parliamentarism. And then there was the bludgeon of physical obstruction. A resolute minority using whistles, trumpets, and tops of desks, to say nothing of vocal chords and fists could create chaos in halls where eloquence and reason were supposed to reign.

The obstruction began as an outburst of the *furor Teutonicus*, as German sacrifices on the altar on Wodan, the thundering Jupiter of the Germanic Olympus. It was an anti-Czech movement with a generous dose of anti-Semitism injected into it by the German extremist groups. But the combination of technical and physical obstruction induced President Abrahamovicz, a Pole of Rumanian extraction, to answer physical violence by an illegal act and by further physical violence. In the beginning, the socialists, internationally minded as they were, could watch the German fury with some detachment. But a breach of the order of business was a different matter. The parliament was the parliament of the privileged classes, but the socialists considered themselves the guardians of parliamentarism, which, via future introduction of the general franchise, was expected one day to carry the labor movement to the pinnacle of power and to far-reaching reforms. They reacted violently and so did the parliamentary authorities. The expulsion of socialist deputies from the chamber by the police brought the masses of workers into the streets. Violent demonstrations and clashes with the police occurred. Suddenly, revolution seemed in the air. That did it, and the Emperor accepted Badeni's resignation.

But what about the decrees? The next ministry (Baron Gautsch) weakened the Badeni decrees somewhat (March 1898), and in the following year, after the intermezzo of still another cabinet, Count Clary finally withdrew them altogether (October 14, 1898), thus restoring the status quo ante Badeni. The years that followed Badeni's departure were filled with all sorts of tumultuous events, including a peasant uprising and pogroms in Galicia. But all this was overshadowed by the continued obstruction in the parliament, except that its actors—and heroes—had changed. Now it was the Czechs who carried on the obstructive tactics, revealing themselves as highly talented and efficient disciples of the Germans from whom they had learnt the art. Only then it began to dawn on the Germans, who liked to think of Austria as *their* state, what fatal precedents had been created by their outbursts of uncontrolled fury. At any rate, the parliamentary machine was again brought to a standstill and legislative acts had to be issued, some of them in a constitutionally questionable way, on the basis of the emergency article 14. Strife among the nationalities, above all between the Germans and the Czechs, appeared to threaten the

20

cohesion and, in fact, the continued existence of the state, let alone the position of the Monarchy as a Great Power.

The conflict grew more and more bitter from month to month. The tactics pursued and the language used grew more and more violent. The Czechs continued to denounce the "crime of October 14," and, since the restoration of the Badeni decrees was not within the purvue of practical politics, no end of the struggle was in sight. This was the situation in which Ernest von Koerber assumed the thankless task of premiership. Between Taaffe's fall and Koerber's advent to power, six prime ministers—four counts, one baron and one knight—had followed each other. Badeni with his 25 months in office held the record of ministerial longevity, the average period of tenure being almost exactly one year. Was Koerber to push the average even farther down?

Koerber is the central figure, the hero, of these lectures. This raises the difficult question (on which we must touch presently) whether he was the *sole* hero of his own policies and of his own era. Whatever the answer, the first thing to be said in introducing Koerber is that he was an unusual figure in the high office. This is, in the first instance, a negative point, referring to what Koerber was *not*. The scion of a military family on his father's side (the grandfather had been a Field Marshal Lieutenant) and of a civil servant family on the distaff side, Koerber, despite the modest "von" that preceded his name, was, if not altogether a commoner, the first non-aristocrat to occupy the position of the presidency of the council of ministers (at least for any significant length of time). As such he was a man of achieved rather than ascribed status. Born in 1850 in Trentino (Trient) in the Italian South Tyrol (which probably accounts for the *semi-Italian* form of his Christian name), Koerber was in his fiftieth year at the time of his appointment, when he was looking back upon a long and successful career as a civil servant. The early stages of this career may have been favored by Koerber's having been a graduate of the *Theresianum*. If old Austria had a counterpart of Eton and Harrow, *Theresianum* was it. By contrast, his doctorate of law was the usual degree acquired by civil servants.

Following his schooling were long years (more than two dec-

21

ades) in the Ministry of Commerce, where Koerber acquired considerable expert knowledge of tariffs, shipping, and finally of railroads. He was very active in helping to create the Ministry of Railroads (1895), which was pared out from the Ministry of Commerce, and then he became the director general of Austrian state railroads. Under Badeni, Koerber became *Sektionschef*, the highest civil servant, in the Ministry of Interior. In the following years he began his political career, first as Minister of Commerce (under Gautsch) and then as Minister of Interior (under Clary). In the last position he had to co-sign (with the rest of the cabinet) the decree which rescinded the Badeni decrees, a circumstance well noted and remembered by the Czechs and, as such, not exactly designed to promote friendly relations with Czech parliamentarians and the Czech public opinion.

Thus Koerber's appointment was an unusual one not merely because he was neither a prince nor a count as had been most of his predecessors. Brief as the foregoing sketch of his career is,[7] it serves to indicate that with Koerber the government was placed in the hands of a man who had accumulated an enormous body of experience as a civil servant. In fact, there were few men, even among the highest civil servants, who could match Koerber's mastery of the administrative machinery, both in the large and in small details, and in particular who rivaled his knowledge and understanding of economic problems. After a long succession of amateurs and dilettantes who carried the burden of the office with easygoing and lighthearted irresponsibility and had to rely intuitively and uncertainly on expert advice, here was a man who was

[7] For data on Koerber's biography, see Heinrich Friedjung "Ernest von Koerber," *Neue oesterreichische Biographie, 1815-1908*, Vienna, 1923, Vol. I, pp. 23-24; Alexander Novotny, "Ernest von Koerber (1850-1919)" in P. Hugo Hantsch, ed., *Gestalter der Geschicke Oesterreichs*, Innsbruck, Vienna, Munich, 1962, p. 487; Robert Ehrhardt, *Im Dienst des alten Oesterreich*, Vienna, 1958, pp. 359-361; Herwig Leitgeb, "Die Ministerpraesidentschaft Dr. Ernest von Koerbers in den Jahren 1900-1904 and Oktober-December 1916" (unpublished doctoral dissertation, 1951), Nationalbibliothek, Vienna, pp. 1-8; Erich Graf Kielmansegg, *Kaiserhaus, Staatsmaenner und Politiker*, Vienna and Munich, 1966, pp. 225, 287-301; Alfred Ableitinger, *Ernest von Koerber und das Verfassungsproblem im Jahre 1900*, Vienna, 1973; Lorenz, "Ernest von Koerber," *Oesterreichisches Biographisches Lexikon, 1815-1950*, Vienna, 1969, Vol. IV, p. 44.

himself an incomparable expert. In addition to his vast experience, Koerber had the gift of quick perception and was remarkable for truly indefatigable industry, or rather, for an insatiable appetite for work. Hence arose his great versatility, which astonished all who came into contact with the man. Koerber, the *Ministerpraesident*, was, therefore, an innovation, and it is not surprising that innovation was paramount in his mind as he took over the reins of power.

A man of this background and character could neither acquiesce in a "muddling through" policy à la Taaffe nor engage in impulsive gambles à la Badeni. Koerber needed a well-considered long-run program, which in itself was novelty. As is true of many significant new ideas, Koerber's innovating thought was simple and in some sense perhaps obvious. It can, therefore, be summarized rather briefly. The immediate task was, of course, to rescue the country from the quagmire of the nationality strife. This was what Koerber's Sovereign expected from the new cabinet. A direct attack on the problem could not be avoided, and Koerber planned to bring the warring parties together in special "mutual understanding" conferences with a view to moving toward a permanent settlement that should be achieved not by a fleeting and easily rescindable decree, but by a law to be duly passed by the parliament and to remain lastingly engraved in the statute book. Thus Koerber took office armed with a carefully prepared bill that was based on a detailed study, district by district, of the Czech provinces and was to serve as the basis for the compromise Koerber hoped to attain.

But the direct approach was not the crux of Koerber's program. The main goal was to engineer a radical shift in political emphasis away from the highly divisive nationality problem and toward a common concern that would unite, coalesce, and integrate all the nationalities of Cisleithania. That "concern" was to be the economic interests.

Accordingly, upon his access to office, Koerber issued in the press a declaration that inter alia contained the following passages: "The national struggles in their very nature and particularly so because of their deplorably long duration have forced the spirits into a onesided passional attitude. In this way, those struggles have paralyzed popular energies from which productive labor could have been expected; they have damaged social intercourse and have even pushed into the background such interests as are common to all the nationalities of the State. . . . The action of the government in the political field proper will be accompanied *pari passu* by lively initiatives in other areas. It is the economic conditions that call specifically for closest possible attention. Despite the presence of abundant preconditions the development of our productive activities has been greatly impeded and has suffered grievously from the consequences of the continuing nationality strife. At a time when in the whole world the industrial upswing means intensification of effort and unification of forces, with us such forces are rendered lame by nationalist strife. To set them free and to place them in the service of welfare and social progress in the State as a whole is a thought that must warm every patriotic heart. Our task is to create for our State a period of repose. . . ."

A few weeks later, Koerber reiterated the idea briefly in his introductory address to the Czech-German "Language Conference" (February 5, 1900). There he stressed that the population, and particularly those strata whose livelihood depended on their labor, was tired of the hopeless struggles and demanded change and positive activity. Koerber concluded his speech by saying: "The goal that this government has fastened its sights upon is to place the full power of the State in the service of culture and national economy."

Finally, both houses of Parliament convened on February 22, 1900. Koerber introduced his cabinet to them and presented his program. As far as the composition of the cabinet was concerned, it should be mentioned that Koerber also took over the Ministry of the Interior, while the Ministry of Finance was entrusted to the celebrated Austrian economist, Eugen von Boehm-Bawerk, and the Ministry of Commerce went to Baron Guido von Call. As we shall show later, the choice of Boehm-Bawerk, very favorably received because of the man's great talents and administrative experience, was to prove a rather fateful one.

The program as announced to the lower chamber revolved around the basic ideas mentioned above, but unlike the previous

24

statements it contained in its references to the budget concrete measures of policies. The relevant passages deserve to be summarized rather fully. In listing the public investments that are not "postponable" or "deferrable" Koerber mentioned the construction of a second railroad connection with the port city of Triest, the railroad to cross both the central granite chain of the Alps (*Tauern*) as well as the parallel mighty southern limestone chain (*Karawanken*); furthermore a railroad to cross a mountain pass in Upper Austria was to establish a shorter connection between Bohemia and Triest; finally, in addition to some local railroads, there was to be a railroad constructed in Galicia connecting the city of Lemberg with the Hungarian plain on the other side of the Carpathian mountains. The aggregate cost of these public works, Koerber estimated, would amount to about half a billion of crowns. But the program was to be even more comprehensive. The extent to which construction of new inland waterways (canals) should be dedicated to the same purpose, Koerber said rather indefinitely, was still under study. But he insisted that regulation of navigable rivers, particularly of those where the cost of carriage of bulky commodities could be decreased, must be included among the urgent tasks of the administration. Thereupon he referred to the need of modernizing the port of Triest, which was far and away Austria's most important sea outlet. To crown the program the Premier referred to industry as the decisive factor in building the economy and promised submission at an early period of time of a bill designed to *promote* industry. A shorter, but essentially the same version of the speech was presented to the First Chamber of the Parliament (*Herrenhaus*).[8]

Thus what Koerber presented to the Parliament was nothing less than a *program for economic development*, as we must call it now, even though the term was not at all in current usage at that time. And, what is more, it was to be a spurt of economic devel-

[8] For the quotations in the preceding four or five paragraphs see Gustav Kolmer, *Parlament und Verfassung in Oesterreich*, Vol. VIII, *1900-1904*, Vienna and Leipzig, 1914, pp. 2-3, 7, 18-19, 22-24; *Stenographisches Protokoll, Haus der Abgeordneten*, Session XVI, Meeting 34, February 22, 1900, pp. 2114-2116. For the texts of the aforementioned bills see *Stenographisches Protokoll, loc. cit.*, Beilagen, Numbers 485 and 526.

opment initiated and carried out by the state, relying largely on what in a less than perfectly felicitous phrase is called "social overhead capital." Note, however, that at the time Koerber communicated his program to the Parliament, an essential and quantitatively large part of it (inland waterways) was still at an inchoate stage of general cogitations and considerations, and the government for the time being had abstained from submitting a bill with concrete technological and financial elaborations of the subject. This may not have been irreparable, but it was a rather serious error of tactics and strategy, unnecessarily diminishing the apparent magnitude and importance of the program.

This error was all the more important in view of the blending of the negative and positive goals of the government program. It was not and could not be a program of economic development pure and simple, that is to say, a program that was of great value in itself. But along with the aim of economic growth or, in Koerber's terms, of increase of well-being (*Wohlstand*), there was the negative aim of removing the parliamentary chaos and making it possible for the Parliament to pass crucial bills such as the budget, the numbers of recruits to be conscripted, and the compact with Hungary. Those things were called public necessities and had to be accomplished quite independently of whether the budget did or did not include items bearing on economic development. As said before, it was the inability of the Czechs and the Germans to agree on the questions of language as well as on the power questions either actually involved or at least suspected to be involved in the linguistic struggles that had condemned the parliament to the helpless state of inactivity. Thus the success of Koerber's program was not to be measured, as would have been natural, merely in terms of increasing the country's wealth and income, but just as much in terms of the government's ability to ensure the normal functioning of the parliament. In fact, under these conditions, it may have appeared that economic development was subsidiary to the second aim and as such as something the importance of which was not to be judged rather highly.

It is, therefore, not surprising that the parliamentary reaction to the Premier's announcement of his policy was not marked by any outbursts of enthusiasm for economic development. As one looks through the pages of the stenographic records that are filled by the debates over Koerber's statement, one finds that most speakers, after expressing cool interest, or even disbelief in the seriousness of Koerber's economic program, quickly turned to the dogmatic discussion of the language problem or, representing the liberal point of view of the time, complained of the inefficiency involved in the activities of bureaucracy in the economic field.[9] In addition, there was the dogmatic rejection of the Investment Bill by the radical Czechs. "Half a billion crowns can only be granted to a government that deserves it. . . . The purpose of our obstruction is to concentrate on things the Government needs most. Hence we shall obstruct the Investment Bill." Besides, Koerber's signature as Minister of the Interior appeared on the previously mentioned Clary's decree, and the Czechs still clamored for atonement for that sin in the commission of which Koerber had taken part.[10] We shall see that it took some time before this attitude was rather radically changed. More than a full year, to be precise. This delay constitutes a historical problem to which some attention must be devoted.

One approach to the problem may lead to the attitude of the Austrian Social-Democratic party and its reaction to Koerber's policy, as expressed in the statements of the undisputed leader of the party, Victor Adler. This calls for an introductory digression. Almost a decade earlier, December 29, 1891, Victor Adler in a letter to Engels complained of the "creeping crisis" in Austria, unemployment, and falling wages. Several months later, August 25, 1892, in a change of mood and of the appraisal of the economic situation, Adler wrote to the same correspondent: "The economic backwardness of the country disappears, one might say, hourly, and we have the advantage that our proletariat is spiritually ahead of the economic development, thanks to the neighborhood of Germany. It is also important that our *hinterland*, Hungary, advances rapidly. *Hungarian industry is being raised by the State*, and so the soil for our movement is officially wid-

---

[9] *Stenographisches Protokoll*, *loc. cit.*, Meetings 38-40, particularly pp. 2503-2505, 2507, 2639.

[10] Josef Penižek, *Aus bewegten Zeiten, 1895-1905*, Vienna, 1906, pp. 213, 219.

ened there and kept in the state of nationalist fever. This is all the more important as we used to have the Slovaks coming to us from Hungary and depressing our standard of living. But now they can be used in Hungary and will soon become entirely different people." Engels replied at once (August 30, 1892): "I am enormously pleased by what you are saying about the rapid industrial progress in Austria and Hungary. *This is the only solid basis for the progress of our movement.*"[11]

It is irrelevant in our context that Adler exaggerated the very brief improvement in Austria's economic conditions that occurred in 1892. What does matter are two things: first, Adler was quite aware of the government-promoted process of industrialization in Hungary and of its beneficial effects for the Social-Democratic labor movement there; and, second, that Engels, to whom Adler as every other socialist leader of the time looked in veneration for guidance and counsel, confirmed Adler's attitude in a strong lapidary sentence that was obviously related to the basic Marxian postulates regarding connection between industrialization and growth of labor movement. One might have expected, therefore, that Adler would greet Koerber's emphasis on economic development and industrialization with considerable interest, if not perhaps with enthusiastic approval.

Accordingly, it is intriguing and somewhat incomprehensible to read Victor Adler's speech before the party congress in the fall (September) of 1900. He said there: "So far Herr Koerber has had no ideas, and there is no danger whatsoever that he may get any ideas in the near future." The position of Social-Democracy as the party of fundamental opposition may explain something, but hardly that charge of lack of ideas addressed to a Prime Minister who entered his office armed with a great and novel idea. And yet to ignore the fact completely and hiding behind the screen of irony was too difficult, and so Adler went on in the same speech: "We, Social-Democrats, place economic demands in the foreground. But when we do it and when the government stresses economic necessities—these are two totally different matters. When Herr

[11] Victor Adler, *Aufsaetze, Reden und Briefe*, Book I: *Victor Adler und Friedrich Engels*, Vienna, 1922, pp. 30-31, 44-45. Italics supplied.

von Koerber makes so many promises, this is meant as a device to induce the political parties to change from their nationalistic policies to another policy hostile to the People. Should the Parliament start functioning again, then the first result would be not to satisfy the needs of the Peoples, but to accept the noxious and for Austria outright fatal compact with Hungary . . . delivering the industrial population of Austria, hands tied, to the Austrian and Hungarian agrarians."[12]

Clearly, Adler refused to take Koerber's ideas regarding economic development and industrialization in the spirit of his correspondence with Engels and in a way that should have been natural for the leader of a party and for the party itself, which proudly regarded itself as Marxian, a term that, when the century was very young, was infinitely clearer and better defined than it has become in our own days. By 1900, the raging debates in Germany on Revisionism cast some doubts on orthodox Marxism, but not within the context that is relevant here and at any rate not within the boundaries of Austria. How negative was the Socialist reaction to Koerber's plans appears even more clearly from the electoral manifesto of the Social-Democratic party (October 1900), which castigated the parliamentary "marasmus" in a "state that is unable to die, but has no force to live," and continued: "The rulers seem to make people forget the necessity to make earnest decisions by having recourse to the petty arts and the shabby tricks of traditional politics."[13] It is in these sneering and debasing terms that reference was made to Koerber's economic plans. The language was unfair and incorrect, because there was nothing "traditional" about those plans.

The attitude of the Socialists, negative as it was, is certainly important for the understanding of Koerber's position in the first year of his government and of the delay alluded to before. Yet a good deal more must be said on the subject than remarks on the negativism and perhaps obtuseness of the Social Democracy that made it disregard its own long-term interests, enlightenedly un-

[12] Victor Adler *op. cit.*, Book VIII: *Victor Adler als Parteimann*, Vienna, 1929, pp. 206, 208.

[13] Ludwig Bruegel, *Geschichte der oesterreichischen Sozialdemokratie*, Vienna, 1923, Vol. IV, p. 340.

derstood. Other events and possibly Koerber's own other plans and errors of omission should be considered.

First of all, there is the question whether Koerber had introduced his economic plans with enough "fanfare," using the term in its most positive connotations. By all accounts, Koerber was a great speaker. No piece written on Koerber by a contemporary, be it an obituary, an article, or passages in memoirs, fails to mention Koerber's extraordinary oratorical gifts. But I must confess that, having perused a very large number of Koerber's public utterances, my own impressions are somewhat different. I, too, must admire the precision, the lucidity, perhaps the beauty of his speeches, frequently adorned by memorable felicitous phrases. As a user of the German language, Koerber stood head and shoulders over his predecessors in office. But a great orator? As Cicero liked to explain, a great many things go into the making of a great speaker—intangible things of which voice, tone, rhythm, gesture, bodily motion are but a few and elude entirely the written record of the speech.[14] Take, for example, the concluding paragraph of the speech with which Koerber presented his program to the Lower Chamber of the Parliament. It reads:

> *"Hohes Haus!* The material and cultural problems are knocking violently at the gates of this Empire. The Government may not reject or neglect these problems, because the political and nationality questions have not been solved yet. The government therefore approaches you with the most urgent prayer to reduce the nationality strife that has been going on for such a long time at least to such an extent that beside it a road may remain free for the spiritual and economic development of the State."[15]

The original language no doubt is much better than my translation. But the latter is sufficient to illustrate the point that must be made here. The passage probably was a moving and impressive appeal. And yet, something seems to be terribly wanting. There is no look far into the future, no attempt to paint the years to come in the bright colors of happy anticipations coupled with the certainty

[14] E.g. Cicero, *De Oratore*, I, XXXIV:156.

[15] *Stenographisches Protokoll, Haus der Abgeordneten*, Session XVI, Meeting 34, February 22, 1900, p. 2116.

of successful attainments. Seen in this way, the speech, as were all Koerber's speeches, was very matter of fact. In other words, there was nothing Saint-Simonian about Koerber. Or, in still other words, there was no desire to create what may be called an "industrialization ideology." The point should not be misunderstood. For Koerber was at all times ready to influence the public through the press and innumerable speeches before various non-governmental forums. But at all times he appealed to cold reason rather than emotion. We shall have to return to the problem and must abandon it now with the uncertain but suggestive surmise that a different spiritual stance on Koerber's part might have induced the Social-Democrats to forge out of their own Marxian ideas an "industrialization ideology," as was happening at that very time somewhere else in Europe. A related surmise is that in this case the delay in question might have been shorter.

A further matter must be considered in this connection. Sources dealing with Koerber invariably mention and praise the man's indefatigable industry. There is no question that Koerber was an unbelievably hard worker, yet no one can escape certain limits of time and physique. One must, therefore, take due notice of the manifold matters that called for Koerber's attention during his first year in office and which had nothing to do with his economic plans and must, therefore, be seen as interruptions and deflections, at least one of them self-induced. The following listing is illustrative and does not include everything that might be included.

As Koerber took office, the economy of the country was affected by a coal miners' strike in Bohemia, Moravia, and Silesia. The strike had lasted for weeks, reducing the quantities of coal in storage and threatening a general fuel shortage. Austrian governments had a long tradition of dealing with workers' strikes with suppression by military forces. It was said that in no country in Europe west of Russia had the workers been so readily and so often fired upon by the soldiers. This, however, was not Koerber's way of handling the situation. In the face of a great deal of noisy protests and demands for suppression on the part of the mine owners sitting in the First Chamber (*Herrenhaus*), Koerber refused to follow the traditional line of policy and instead of dispatching soldiers, dispatched his Minister of Justice to the mines. Thereupon a compromise, arrived at in negotiations, ended the strike. The agreements reached served a year later as the basis for a law reducing working hours in the mines (nine hours from portal to portal) and raising the miners' wages. This way of acting was well in line with Koerber's behavior in office both as a Prime Minister and also as Minister of the Interior, who was in charge of the state's means of physical enforcement. More will be said about Koerber's general policies in matters involving the citizens' exercise of constitutional rights. For the moment it will suffice to keep in mind the settlement of the miners' strike as one of the matters that laid claim on Koerber's time and thought and deflected him from pursuing the main line of his policy.

From April till June 1900, Koerber was preoccupied with a strange and rather anachronistic problem. Francis Ferdinand, who had become the Crown Prince (or rather the heir apparent) after the suicide at Mayerling of Crown Prince Rudolph, fell in love with a Countess Chotek and asked the Emperor Francis Joseph for permission to marry the lady. The Emperor refused. Even though the Bohemian nobility of the Choteks went far back into the depth of times, the proposed bride was regarded as *unebenbürtig*, that is to say, of inferior rank in terms of the curiously never published House Laws (*Hausgesetze*) of the Habsburg dynasty. The Prince was given the choice between concluding the proposed marriage and resigning his position. In the case of resignation, the right of succession would devolve upon his younger brother Otto, very properly married to a daughter of the royal house of Saxony. Incidentally, when Otto died a few years later, he was said to have died of a case of extramaritally acquired venereal disease, the virulence of which amazed even an eminent Viennese professor of dermatology, who as "a looker-on here in Vienna" must have seen a great deal in the area of his specialization.[16]

At any rate, Francis Ferdinand, a man of deep Catholic faith, felt he could not resign a post on which he had been placed by the Lord. Accordingly, he bombarded Koerber with pitiful and passionate letters, threatening among other things suicide or insanity

---

[16] Kielmansegg, *Kaiserhaus, Staatsmaenner und Politiker*, p. 141.

and urging the Prime Minister to find a solution that would avoid resignation and permit marriage. It may be noted that the position taken by the Emperor is not easy to understand, and this not simply because it was out of place in the spiritual climate of the last year of the nineteenth century.[17] The Emperor might have considered that the requirement of *Ebenbürtigkeit*, which involved a great deal of inbreeding in royal marriages, is likely to have inflicted considerable damage both at earlier times in the Habsburg dynasty and even in the Emperor's own family, perhaps by the taint or double taint of the genes of the Bavarian Wittelsbach dynasty.[18]

Whether under the pressures of Francis Ferdinand or for other reasons, after many meetings, audiences, conferences and councils, involving also Hungarian government representatives (because the concept of *Ebenbuertigkeit* was alien to Hungarian law), Koerber abandoned his original negative attitude and the permission for the Prince to marry was finally issued on the condition that it was to be a morganatic marriage, excluding the children thereof from the rights of succession in both Austria and Hungary which renunciation the Prince had to affirm by a solemn oath. Much ado about nothing, we may be tempted to say, but for Koerber it had to be a problem of crucial significance.

In the very midst of these goings on, dramatic things were happening in the Parliament. In May 1900, Koerber submitted to the Parliament the bills concerning regulation of the language problems in Bohemia and Moravia. For the purposes of the main

[17] But the sentence in the text may be ill-founded. An Austrian historian writing in the 1970s does not hesitate to speak of "the marriage of Archduke Francis Ferdinand with a *totally morganatic (einer ganz unebenbuertigen)* Bohemian countess" (sic). Thus Countess Chotek to the mind of an Austrian of today seems to have been the ultimate in "morganatics." See Ableitinger, *Ernest von Koerber und das Verfassungsproblem im Jahre 1900.* This book will be referred to presently at some length.

[18] It remains an open question whether circumstances of this kind had anything to do with the suicide of Crown Prince Rudolph in 1899. Richard Barkeley, *The Road to Mayerling,* New York, 1958, pp. 98-99. Note also the opinion of Josef Breuer, who had stood beside Freud at the cradle of psychoanalysis; Robert Kann, ed., *Marie von Ebner-Eschenbach–Dr. Josef Breuer, Ein Briefwechsel 1889-1916,* Vienna, 1969, p. 154.

theme of these lectures it is not necessary here to go into the contents of these bills. Suffice it to say that they were based on an extremely detailed knowledge of the relevant conditions in the two provinces, had been deeply thought out, lucidly and carefully phrased, and that their emphasis on local district governments (*Kreise*) constituted a treatment of the problems involved that was exceedingly fair to all parties concerned. It is probably correct to say that the bills did not contain any ideas that had not been floating around in previous debates and cogitations, but it is just as correct to note that for the first time the Parliament received an opportunity to settle the matter by law in such comprehensive and far-reaching fashion.

Nevertheless Koerber had hardly finished his speech introducing the bills when the Czech speaker rose to announce the continuation of obstruction. The reasons for this decision of the Czech faction are not easy to disentangle, having been partly substantive and partly matters of prestige and power. It was said the Czechs objected to the failure of the bills to stipulate Czech "internal" language for the *whole* of Bohemia, and that the bills, by reducing the role of the provincial governors, unduly increased the part to be played by the ministries in Vienna. It was further said that the Czechs were moved by the desire to show that Czech obstruction could be every bit as effective as the German obstruction against Badeni had been. It was also argued that the purpose of the continued obstruction was to strengthen the Austrian state by insisting on the constitutionally granted equality of all the languages of the Monarchy. These and many other more or less plausible and implausible things were said.

At any rate, the obstruction started as technical obstruction involving perpetual "motions for urgency, continued roll calls, readings and rereadings of additional rather wilful motions and using to the hilt all the opportunities provided by the order of business." But then after a period during which the Parliament had been prorogued, filibuster degenerated into physical obstruction, producing acoustic effects fully as good as anything earlier described in this lecture. On June 6, Koerber made a serious appeal to the lower chamber. He still expressed the hope that parties would be amenable to moderation. But he added: "This is truly

34

the last hour in which we express this hope. If it remains unredeemed, then we (the Government) shall face the compelling necessity to lead the State out of the pernicious strife and to lay free an area for the economic work which the population wishes."[19] This was a clear threat with an unconstitutional recourse to article 14, in other words with a coup d'état. The obstruction continued, and two days later, just before midnight, Koerber went to the Emperor for authorization and returned to the continuing frenzy in the Parliament to announce the closing of the session.

How are these events to be interpreted? As a failure of Koerber's? It seems that this was the prevailing view of his contemporaries, traces of which are still visible in literature.[20] The situation, however, was more complicated than it appeared superficially. First of all, it should be noted that closing the session and even dissolving the Parliament and the Emperor's oral authorization thereto, had been one of the secret conditions of Koerber's accepting the Prime Ministry and was explicitly laid down in the secret audiences that preceded the appointment. It is even possible that Koerber had had a signed authorization in his files from the beginning and that the midnight trip to the palace, involving waking up the sleeping Emperor, was nothing but a well-acted play, designed to make a dramatic impact upon public opinion and to demonstrate the government's ability to act with decisive and surprising force.[21]

Second, Koerber apparently had still another arrow in his quiver. One must go back to the discussions between Koerber and his main aide and adviser, Rudolf Sieghart, prior to Koerber's becoming Prime Minister. At that time, it was clearly mentioned that, should the attempts at straightening out the differences between the Czechs and the Germans fail, a threefold coup d'état should be carried out by the Emperor's fiat involving (1) introduction of a democratic electoral reform, (2) regulation of the

[19] Gustav Kolmer, *Parlament und Verfassung*, Vol. VIII, pp. 104-105.

[20] *Ibid.*, p. 108, and Heinrich Friedjung, "Ernest von Koerber," *Neue oesterreichische Biographie*, Vol. I, Vienna, 1923, p. 26.

[21] Cf. Rudolf Sieghart, *Die letzten Jahrzehnte einer Grossmacht*, Berlin, 1932, pp. 40, 43-44.

language problem, and (3) reform of the parliamentary order of business that would preclude obstruction.[22] Yet no agreement along these lines was ever obtained from the Emperor. Recently an undated memorandum in Koerber's hand has been discovered in the archives by Alfred Ableitinger, who was inspired by the discovery to compose a book on the subject.[23] The document does indeed propose solving the parliamentary problems by the avowedly unconstitutional imposition of reforms in three areas mentioned. The author supposes that the memorandum was submitted by Koerber to the Emperor sometime during the summer of 1900.

Because Ableitinger's book on this subject bears on the problems treated in these lectures, a few critical remarks concerning it may well be in order. The author's main point, if I understand him correctly, is that it is not the measures of economic policy, but precisely the coup d'état plans that should be regarded as the actual cynosure of Koerber's program. Moved by this thought, Ableitinger betrays neither interest in, nor understanding for, economic problems in general and the relevant Koerber plans in particular. Besides, by confining his treatment to the single year 1900, he precluded any comprehensive appreciation of the "Koerber era."

Among Koerber's three proposals for reform to be imposed in an extra-parliamentary manner, disregarding the provisions of the constitution,[24] far and away the most interesting concerns the electoral reform. The Austrian electoral system was strictly a four-class system of highly privileged voters to which Badeni had added a fifth, so-called general class (or *Kurie*) of manhood franchise. The general class was assigned about 16 percent of seats in the chamber and about 36 percent of its voters also voted in their own respective classes. Thus, the democratic element injected into the system by Badeni was picayune indeed, and the introduction of general and equal suffrage remained the central political

---

[22] *Ibid.*, p. 40.

[23] Ableitinger, *Ernest von Koerber und das Verfassungsproblem im Jahre 1900.*

[24] In the Austrian political lingo, this method was called an "octroi," the term having acquired specific Austrian connotations.

demand of the Austrian labor movement. Koerber's proposals fell far short of satisfying that demand, but involved highly significant concessions to it. Koerber's franchise would remain a class system, in which 20 percent of the seats would be assigned to the highest tax payers, another 20 percent to the most educated stratum, and finally 60 percent to a truly general class in which literacy and a three months' residence were to be the only prerequisites for exercising the right of franchise.

This proposal is of considerable interest in the present context because it is closely connected with the economic plans of the Prime Minister. The two privileged classes preserved in Koerber's electoral system can be described as representing "economy" and "culture," the two terms that Koerber in his speeches regularly juxtaposed. In particular, in Koerber's mind the class of the highest taxpayers should represent "the economically active population," the term Koerber used to describe the entrepreneurs, particularly in industry and banking. Thus, the two classes were thought to constitute the basis of a new political party, the "Economic Party," which would have complete understanding for the policies of economic development. The idea and the term of "Economic Party" apparently was used by Theodor Herzl in his conversations with Koerber in April 1900.[25]

At the same time, however, the establishment of a truly general class which was supposed to have the majority in the Parliament also had strong leanings toward greater stress on economic policy. For the memorandum included Koerber's analysis of the Social-Democratic party, which would be the main beneficiary of the establishment of the general class. Here Koerber, with astonishing knowledgeability and understanding, tried to explain to the Emperor that the party was in the process of shedding revolutionary methods and wished to attain its aims by legal means; that the very international position of the party made it an opponent of any extreme nationalism; and, finally, that the membership of the party, because of its economic condition, was most interested in economic progress. In Koerber's view, therefore, Social Democ-

[25] Theodor Herzl, *Tagebuecher*, Berlin, 1925, Vol. II, p. 417.

racy was to be regarded as a reliable support of the state.[26] The preceding is the most significant portion of Koerber's memorandum. Ableitinger, however, fascinated by the constitutional problem of the coup d'état, fails to pay attention to the connections between those plans and Koerber's economic policy.

As far as the coup d'état, or the *"octroi,"* plans were concerned, the matter came to an abrupt end at the meeting of the Crown Council (*Kronrat*) in September 1900, where the Hungarian Prime Minister opposed any such action in Cisleithania, because it would render the whole constitutional coexistence of the two "halves" of the Monarchy highly problematic. Besides, it was clear that the ruling class in Hungary apprehended that general franchise in Austria would raise the same problem in Hungary, where democratic suffrage would undermine the position of that class and make its continued rule over non-Hungarian nationalities well-nigh impossible. With the rejection of the plans by the Crown Council, Ableitinger tells us, "Koerber's great game had failed."[27] Less than one year later, the Emperor ordered all the documents related to the plans to be sent to the files, laid *ad acta*, which, in Austrian bureaucratic language, meant dispatched to the cemetery.[28] Ableitinger speaks also of the "amputation which the failure of the constitutional plans meant for Koerber's policy seen in its totality."[29]

I consider this view untenable. If the "failure" had been as serious as Ableitinger suggests, why did not Koerber then offer his resignation, even though he claimed later that during his period in office he was ever ready to stress to the Emperor his readiness to go?[30] And the answer to this question should be obvious. The "octroi" plans were not Koerber's "great game." The whole story was no more than an insignificant episode within the

---

[26] Cf. Ableitinger, *Ernest von Koerber*, pp. 186-188. It is hardly very sensible when Ableitinger, in discussing this point, brings in Metternich, of all people, and tries to argue that Koerber's positive attitude toward Social Democracy was similar "after 50 or 60 years" to Metternich's view of the loyal attitudes of the plebs. The purpose of this willful and implausible dragging in of Metternich presumably is to cast an unfavorable light on Koerber.

[27] *Ibid.*, p. 176, "grosses Spiel gescheitert."

[28] *Ibid.*   [29] *Ibid.*, p. 221.

[30] Cf. Josef Redlich, *Schicksalsjahre Oesterreiches, 1908-1919, Das politische Tagebuch*, Graz-Cologne, 1953, Vol. I, p. 28.

great historical episode of Koerber's ministry. Even Ableitinger seems to have an inkling of the truth, when, after all the big words of "amputation" and "failure," he squeezes in (in a dependent clause) an admittedly vaguely phrased reference to Koerber's economic plans; and then proceeds to speak of Koerber's belief in the objective integrating power of economic development.[31] This is fine, except that, appearing as an afterthought, these admissions destroy the thesis of the book. Thus, instead of resigning, Koerber proceeded to dissolve the Parliament, whose session had been closed in June and left the legislative problem to the newly elected Reichsrat that was to convene in 1901.

Thus, the problem as to why Koerber allowed the year 1900 to pass without concentrating more than he did on the economic problem finds some explanation in the numerous competing matters to which the attention of the Prime Minister had to be given. It is also possible that, in view of the planned dissolution of the Parliament, Koerber thought it wiser to postpone a full attack on the front of economic development until after the election. The composition of the new Reichsrat, it is true, could not be exactly foreseen, and further radicalization of the membership was altogether possible. But as early as December 1899 it had been stated in the conversations with Sieghart that "radical deputies . . . are much more grateful for economic measures than the representatives of the bourgeoisie."[32] This thought agreed completely with what Koerber several months later wrote in his evaluation of the Social-Democratic party. Koerber had not ignored economic development altogether during that year. On the contrary, there was a rich flow of Koerber's statements to the press, and he made many speeches on economic problems to various businessmen's associations. And yet, one must wonder why Koerber had abstained in the early months of 1900 from presenting to the Parliament a bill on investment in canals and river regulations. Nor, as we shall see, is there evidence that the following months were used for an intensive study of those projects. It is just possible that here lay a serious error of omission.

We return at length to the previously raised question whether Koerber alone must be considered the father of his ideas. A dis-

---

[31] Ableitinger, *Ernest von Koerber*, p. 221.

[32] Rudolf Sieghart, *Die letzten Jahrzehnte einer Grossmacht*, p. 40.

cussion of the problem requires the introduction of a curious, controversial, and imposing figure: Rudolf Sieghart. Sieghart, like many other notable figures on the Viennese scene, came to the capital from Austrian Silesia as an impecunious young man to study law and economics. He studied under Carl Menger, the creator of the Austrian School of Economics, and under Anton Menger, who taught civil law procedure (*Zivilprozess*) but at the same time, along with his rather dry main subject, was engaged in a number of exciting studies dealing with social problems and problems of socialism. As Sieghart summarized the influence of the two men upon him, he had learnt from Carl Menger the methods of economics, while the scholarly problems that he approached came from Carl's brother, Anton. And indeed among the numerous scholarly publications of young Sieghart was a highly sympathetic essay on Gall, an interesting, but forgotten, figure in the earlier history of German socialism. For those who knew Sieghart's activities during the 1920s in the First Austrian Republic and regarded him as a rabid opponent of Austrian socialists, his early social views will come as a surprise. But this is not the end of inconsistencies and surprises. The man whose first job and political apprenticeship were served in the office of the Liberal party later became closely allied with the Catholic Christian-Social party, to whom political and economic liberalism was gall and wormwood. In the highly anti-Semitic milieu and climate of Vienna of the period, Sieghart, the son of a rabbi, managed to acquire a position that gave him a strong part in regulating the pre-conditions for the previously mentioned marriage of the heir apparent and, by the same token, in determining who should be the future Emperor of the country. Sieghart was able then and for years later to exert powerful influence in choosing the members of the cabinet in Austria. There is little doubt that Sieghart was a man of extraordinary abilities that were coupled with an enormous industry. In 1895 (as a man of 29), Sieghart began his career as civil servant in the Ministry of Finance, working under the great Austrian economist, Boehm-Bawerk, on direct taxation and also concerning himself theoretically and practically with the cartel legislation.[33]

[33] It may be added that Sieghart, who at the start of his career showed great

40

The fateful connection between Koerber and Sieghart began in December 1899 in proper Viennese fashion when Koerber, engaged in the usual lunchtime promenade through the streets of the Inner City, met Sieghart by accident, asked to accompany him, and inquired about Sieghart's general views of the political situation. According to Sieghart's description, he was able to serve up on the spot a well thought-out plan that included the idea of a political truce to be utilized to move economic problems into the foreground. "Koerber seemed to like this program."[34] At the conclusion of the walk, Koerber expressed the desire to remain in contact with Sieghart. A few years earlier Sieghart had left the Ministry of Finance and entered the Press Department of the Prime Minister's office (*Ministerratspraesidium*), where excerpts from newspapers were prepared for the Emperor. This job gave Sieghart plenty of time for scholarly writings, on the strength of which he had become *Privatdozent* at the University of Vienna, that is to say, received the *venia legendi* there. But now the time of leisure in office was over. Koerber saw to it that Sieghart received instant promotion and brought him into his immediate vicinity, which marked the beginning of Sieghart's meteoric career as a civil servant, of his rise to enormous power, and also of the transformation of the Prime Minister's office into the very center of governmental activities, at the expense of the position and the weight of the individual ministries.

To what extent was Sieghart the originator or co-originator of Koerber's ideas? The question defies an easy and unambiguous answer. The previously mentioned historian, Alfred Ableitinger, wrote his Ph.D. thesis on the subject. In this work the author makes the following statement: "The main task of the present study is to determine the share of Rudolf Sieghart's personal ideas and views in the formulation of Austrian domestic policy and the measure of his personal co-operation in the execution of that pol-

---

interest in the history of socialism, in his old age let his bank finance the private military troops of Austrian fascism and their attacks upon Austrian democracy. This was the last paradoxical frill placed upon the surprises and inconsistencies mentioned in the text. The destinies of men! See Karl Ausch, *Als die Banken fielen, Zur Soziologie der politischen Korruption*, Vienna-Zurich, 1968, p. 3; Jacques Hannak, *Im Sturm eines Jahrhunderts*, Vienna, 1952, p. 360.

[34] Cf. Sieghart, *Die letzten Jahrzehnte einer Grossmacht*, pp. 36-37.

icy. For both that share and that measure are controversial."[35]
This no doubt is the proper question to ask. Unfortunately, the
author is unable, in the 300-odd pages of his thesis, to provide a
satisfactory answer. And this is so for good and not so good reasons. Most of the files of the Prime Ministry, except for some
scorched papers, perished in the fire of the Palace of Justice in
Vienna on July 15, 1927. In addition, Sieghart's own papers were
impounded or lost in 1938 after Hitler's invasion of Austria. This
means that the only real source available is the previously quoted
volume of Sieghart's memoirs, which includes among other
things excerpts from his diaries. Only sporadically could Ableitinger check on the accuracy of the memoirs. It is certainly not
without significance that his conclusion was quite positive, and he
was quite willing to regard the memoirs as a reliable historical
source.[36] The only thing that weakens this conclusion for our purposes is Ableitinger's stress on political and, in spots, intellectual
history, and his rather complete lack of interest and understanding
of economic problems. This lack of comprehension goes so far
that Ableitinger at one point does not hesitate to say that "the *only*
[*sic*] thing that was new [in Koerber's program] was Koerber's
method of convening formal conciliation conferences," thus
thoughtlessly eliminating the Prince of Denmark from the play.[37]
Thus we must rely on our own reading and interpretation of the
memoirs.

Sieghart's description of the program he outlined during his
walk with Koerber is not an excerpt of the diary; the style of
Sieghart's statement with its elegant puns bears the marks of subsequent editing. Nor is it likely that Koerber, the eager conver-
sationalist, listened to a long monologue without inserting
thoughts and remarks of his own. And there was too much in the
monologue aside from the stress on importance of economic
policies. There was the idea of conciliation conferences and the
stress on the necessity of dealing with the language problem by
law rather than by decree. It is difficult, therefore, to stifle the

[35] Alfred Ableitinger, "Rudolf Sieghart (1866-1934) und seine Taetigkeit im
Ministerratspraesidium, ein Beitrag zur Geschichte der oesterreichischen Innen-
politik im ersten Jahrzehnt unseres Jahrhunderts." Unpublished Dissertation,
Graz, 1964, p. 5.

[36] *Ibid.*, pp. 6, 302. [37] *Ibid.*, p. 83.

suspicion that Sieghart's text, written some three decades after the event, is more than a recapitulation of plans and policies to which, more or less passively, more or less actively, in a give and take fashion, Sieghart, from his fertile mind, no doubt made many a contribution.

Sieghart, it is true, was a trained economist. But his teacher, Carl Menger, as the other great figures of the Austrian School of Economics, never showed any interest in the problems of economic growth and development. Nor could interest in problems of this type have been induced by Anton Menger, with his preoccupation with social problems and intellectual history. The years Sieghart spent in the Ministry of Finance were devoted mostly to technical problems of taxation, and his chief there, Boehm-Bawerk, a man of orthodox financial ideas, had as little concern for economic growth as Carl Menger. Finally, there was Ernst von Plener, the great erudite of the Liberal party, whom Sieghart admired. But Plener's erudition extended largely to England, and the idea of a government-created spurt of economic development must have been entirely antagonistic to his mind. Thus Sieghart, both theoretically and practically, was a tyro in matters of economic growth.

Koerber, by contrast, as Sieghart mentions explicitly, "spent half his life in government offices dealing with commerce and railroads." "He knew, therefore, what the situation was like, and received *my ideas* with great understanding."[38] Sieghart goes on to stress his belief that the "intermission" between the dissolution of Parliament and the forgathering of the new chamber should be filled with preparation of, and agitation for, the coming economic measures.[39] This is Sieghart's strongest statement on the subject. Nevertheless, the implied dichotomy: "Sieghart's ideas and Koerber's execution" need not be accepted at face value. Sieghart certainly was Koerber's most gifted and most efficient collaborator. It is well established, for instance, that Koerber's language bills[40] came from Sieghart's pen. Koerber, as Sieghart ad-

---

[38] Rudolf Sieghart, *Die letzten Jahrzehnte einer Grossmacht*, p. 56. Italics supplied.

[39] *Ibid.*

[40] *Vide supra.*

mitted, was never reluctant to give Sieghart credit for his contributions, and he remained loyal to Sieghart for years to come, through all the attacks on Sieghart and all the public hostility to Sieghart. Yet, it was Koerber who, with an imperfectly disguised reference to Sieghart, made the following pronouncement years later: "I have made my policies and also my speeches all by myself."[41]

With this statement, we may leave the problem of Sieghart's role in shaping Koerber's policies which, after all, is a personal side issue rather than an historically significant problem. For the rest, it should be mentioned that the characterization of Koerber in this lecture must remain incomplete inasmuch as nothing has been said on Koerber's actions as an administrator during his years in office when he tried to "modernize" the administration of the country, or rather the social character and the activities of civil servants, particularly in their contacts with the population, and when he tried to change the traditional handling, or rather mishandling, of the laws regarding the freedom of press and assembly. There will be, however, an opportunity later in these lectures to touch on these problems when dealing with Koerber's treatment in literature, including the views of his contemporaries, and also when returning to the appreciation (or the lack of it) of Koerber's policies by the Austrian labor movement, whose attitude on the question enters into a number of factors that were in one way or another connected with the success and failure of Koerber's policies. Here lies a real problem of social, intellectual, and economic history. By his policies Koerber tried to reduce the economic backwardness of the country, which he regarded as a goal worth striving for, quite independently of the positive political by-products that could be attained in the process. And, as has been intimated before, no other group in Austria was both by its ideology and by its interests so well prepared to receive Koerber's message with sympathy, and perhaps enthusiasm. This will become clearer after, in the next lecture, I deal with the central problem of Koerber's policies which, to repeat, was the economic backwardness of Austria.

[41] Josef Redlich, *Schicksaljahre Oesterreichs* (November 5, 1909), pp. 29-30.

The Economic Backwardness of Austria

IN MY APPROACH to the industrial development of Europe before the First World War, I used the concept of the degree of economic backwardness as an organizing principle in a typology of great spurts of industrialization and in attempts to understand the different nature of those spurts as they occurred in the individual European countries. I had, therefore, to consider whether "degree of economic backwardness" was an operational concept and came to the conclusion that, while it defied cardinal measurement, it provided all the operationality needed for ordinal measurement, that is to say, the term enabled us to rank the countries in question along the line of increasing backwardness. And that was fully sufficient for purposes of the historical analysis at hand.[1]

Nevertheless, finding for Cisleithania the correct place on that line encounters some difficulty that deserves to be dealt with explicitly. In this approach, the individual countries, that is to say, states, are used as a unit of observation. In every case of industrialization, there were considerable differences in the rate and nature of industrial progress among the various regions of the country involved. At the same time, however, the faster developing regions received at least labor and frequently also capital and en-

---

[1] Cf. Alexander Gerschenkron, *Economic Backwardness in Historical Perspective*, Cambridge, Massachusetts, 1962, pp. 42-44, and Alexander Gerschenkron, *Europe in the Russian Mirror*, Cambridge University Press, 1970, p. 99. It is unfortunate that Professor Cameron, in criticizing my approach, blandly declares the degree of economic backwardness to be a non-operational concept, without any reference to my distinction between cardinal and ordinal measurements. A critic should read the works he criticizes with more care. See Rondo Cameron, ed., *Banking and Economic Development, Some Lessons of History*, London-Toronto, 1972, p. 14. Professor Cameron goes on wondering whether Sweden was economically as backward as Russia. A superficial acquaintance with the economic history of a country that managed to avoid enserfment of its peasantry or a leafing through the pages of E. F. Heckscher's, *An Economic History of Sweden* would have quickly silenced his wonderments.

trepreneurial talent from the more backward regions. This cannot be said of Austria, where such industrial development as took place concentrated largely in a few central provinces such as Syria and Lower Austria (with some parts of Upper Austria) in the Alps[2] and Bohemia, Moravia, and Silesia in the Sudeten. At the same time, the periphery in the East and the South made very little contribution to the evolution of the more active provinces. Poles and Ruthenians from Galicia and Rumanians from Bukowina did not migrate within the Monarchy, but preferred emigration overseas, and the same was largely true of the Italians in South Tyrol, or the Dalmatians, or Bosnians, and only slightly less true of the Slovenian inhabitants of Carniola. Thus the inclusion of the peripheral areas of Cisleithania made precious little economic sense, so that one has primarily to think of the central provinces. Once this is done, the question whether Austria was more or less backward than Italy can be resolved without difficulty, and Cisleithania, understood in this restricted sense, can be reasonably assigned its place on the aforementioned line between Germany and Italy. This is so with regard to the historically given events, as it were, *de lege lata*, and keeping in mind that *de lege ferenda* the situation may well appear in a different guise, in particular because Koerber's economic plan envisaged in a very important measure the closer economic integration of the peripheral areas into the central areas of Austria. To this aspect of Koerber's plan we shall return briefly when discussing the actual legislative acts that came to be adopted and the actions that were pursued, or failed to be pursued, in its execution.

I have argued that in conditions of "moderate" or "medium" economic backwardness the banks are likely to play considerable part during the great spurt of industrialization in providing the industrial enterprises with both capital and entrepreneurial guidance.[3] On this basis, were I to analyze the history of the great

---

[2] The light industry in Vorarlberg (on the Swiss border) should also be mentioned.

[3] In this connection, I read with some surprise the statement by David F. Good in his interesting article "Stagnation and 'Take-Off' in Austria 1873-1913" (*The Economic History Review*, 2nd series, Vol. XXVII:I, February 1974), according to which I have failed to supply an operational definition of the "great spurt." This is again a case of careless reading of the works criticized. I have said explicitly that

spurt in Austria's industrial history, I should have expected the banks—*qua* investment or promotional banks—to have been of major significance. That was indeed my expectation as I approached the study of Italian industrialization *and after I succeeded in ascertaining a period of a great spurt in that country*. It was gratifying to find that expectation fully verified by the arrival in Italy, and the activities there, of the German investment banks.

But to return to Austria, it should be in order first to refer to an excellent paper by Richard L. Rudolf, which was supposed to function as a "test case" for my approach.[4] Not the least value of this article consists in the inclusion of a year by year index of Austria's industrial output for the years 1880-1913.[5] Nevertheless, a difficulty of mine in this connection should be mentioned.[6]

---

a great spurt is distinguished—and recognizable—by the fact that its intensity is barely affected by an international depression in the midst of it. To that very operational criterion, a number of equally operational structural changes in the course of the great spurt were added. Alexander Gerschenkron, *Economic Backwardness*, pp. 77, 203.

[4] See Richard L. Rudolf, "Austria, 1800-1914," in Rondo Cameron, ed., *Banking*, Chapter II, pp. 27-57.

[5] *Ibid.*, pp. 30-32.

[6] In the manuscript of this book I paid due respect to this truly pioneering effort, but had to criticize—and criticize strongly—the lack of an appendix in which nature of the index, its territorial extent and in particular the dating and character of the weights used would have been explained. Fortunately, I was able at the very last opportunity to delete those strictures from my text. For, just as I was to correct the galley proof, the mail brought me a copy of Rudolf's new book: Richard Rudolf, *Banking and Industrialization in Austria-Hungary*, Cambridge University Press, 1976). While there was no time for me to examine the book, I could go over Appendix A therein, which does contain the explanation of the index that I had so badly missed. I was gratified to note that in constructing his index Rudolf followed closely the methodology I had used in preparing my index of industrial output in Italy. This is properly acknowledged by the author in a footnote on p. 272 of the book. It is pleasant indeed to see that one's work can be put to profitable use by other scholars.

I still would have preferred a fuller appendix. For instance, in addition to the index based on value added weights also the results of using employment and horse powers installed as alternative weights, which the author says (p. 202) he had computed, should have been published. It is awkward to arouse the curiosity of the reader without satisfying it. This is particularly so in this case because alternative results are likely to do more than just provide a check on the main calculation; for such comparisons can make additional contributions to our comprehension

Two: Economic Backwardness

In what sense can Rudolf's paper be regarded as a test case of my approach? It is important to raise the question, because it relates to the appraisal of the position of the Austrian economy at the end of the nineteenth century, that is to say at the time when Koerber entered the stage equipped with his ideas and plans. As one looks through the relevant literature, one may single out for the problem at hand the valuable study by Eduard Maerz.[7]

It is true that Maerz's study is primarily built upon research in the *Austrian Credit Anstalt* and is mainly concerned with the history of that bank. But being such a recent study, the book contains a good deal of general literature about Austrian banking. At the same time, it is regrettable that Professor Maerz did not attempt to provide quantitative answers to highly important historical questions. To give just two or three examples, one cannot learn from the study what was, in different periods, the weight in the aggregate activities of the *Credit Anstalt* of underwriting of government loans and dealing in government bonds, as against the weight of various forms of participation in financing industrial enterprises. And as far as the latter activities were concerned, it would be most enlightening to know how these activities were distributed between heavy and light industries. Finally, it would have been just as important to learn how much of the bank's long-term investment in industrial enterprises was hidden under the guise of short-term, but in reality revolving, current account credits.[8] Providing a basis for answering these questions certainly will raise a

---

of processes of industrialization. As mentioned earlier, there still remains the broad question of suitability in the special conditions of Cisleithenia of using the whole state as a proper unit of observation. (Cf. Herbert Matis, *Oesterreichs Wirtschaft, 1848-1913*, Berlin 1972, p. 393.) Construction of an index confined to the industrial provinces of the country, within which there were plentiful factor movements would still seem very desirable. Cogitations of this sort cannot, of course, diminish the value of Rudolf's trail-blazing performance.

Let me add that with the help of the index of names and subjects I noticed that Rudolf does indeed devote one paragraph to the Koerber experiment, but refrains altogether from discussing its problems which, I suppose, is not surprising in a study whose theme is *banking* (rather than State) and *industrialization*.

[7] Eduard Maerz, *Oesterreichische Industrie- und Bankpolitik in der Zeit Franz Josephs I*, Vienna-Zurich, 1968.

[8] The usage is properly mentioned by Maerz, *ibid.*, p. 109.

host of other exciting historical questions. It is very much to be hoped that Professor Maerz will expand his study in the directions indicated and thus transform it from a useful, factual report into a piece of historical analysis.

What emerges from this and other studies is the indubitable fact of Austrian banks' provision of capital for long-term investment in industry. Nevertheless, one is surprised to find in the concluding pages of Maerz's study the following statement: "One might object that the development described in the preceding (concerning connection of financial and industrial capital proceeded in larger or smaller measure in all modern industrial countries, and that therefore cannot be seen as being characteristic for Austria alone. But there are indications that in no other country the big banks played such a determining role in economic life as they did in the Austrian Monarchy."[9] This statement echoes one made more than half-a-century earlier by the president of another big Austrian bank. "The history of the Anglobank shows that in our fatherland the banks are more closely connected with production than in any other country."[10]

The latter statement, made by a banker on the festive occasion of the semi-secular jubilee of his bank, must not be weighed on pharmaceutical scales. But the generality of the previous assertion by a scholar calls for some critical remarks. First of all, the statement is valueless in that it does not make the basis of comparison at all clear. Is Germany being included in the reference to "other countries," and, if so, is the reference to the policies of German investment banks before or after the crucially separating line that was drawn by the crisis of 1900? Did Professor Maerz have in mind the whole history of his bank or perhaps only the period since the middle of the 1890s when, as he says elsewhere, "profound changes took place in the policies and the practice of Austrian banks" and "a more intimate relation between the world of industry and that of finance *began to develop?*"[11]

[9] *Ibid.*, p. 372.

[10] See Carl Morawitz, *50 Jahre Geschichte einer Wiener Bank*, Vienna, 1914, p. 76.

[11] Eduard Maerz, *Oesterreichische Industrie- und Bankpolitik*, pp. 295, 297. Italics supplied.

Two: Economic Backwardness

Unguarded assertions of this kind do blur problems in which an economic historian should be primarily interested. It is fairly clear, however, that the intensity of the banks' industry relations varied significantly over the second half of the nineteenth century, and particularly that, in the long years between 1873 and 1896, those relations were pursued with great caution and reticence on the part of the banks.[12] But these were precisely the years during which the German banks let their relations with industrial enterprises develop to a high point and accumulated an enormous amount of experience that stood them in such a good stead when it came to a transfer of their "knowhow" to Italy. One must conclude that the long hiatus in Austria and the lateness of the resumption of "intimate relations," correctly registered by Professor Maerz, must be taken as an indicator of Austria's economic backwardness.

There is little doubt that weighty reasons explained the cautious policies of the banks. A complete discussion would take us too far. But some remarks on the problem will lead us to a better understanding of the climate within which Koerber matured his plans. First of all, one must mention the impact of the crisis of 1873 and the revulsion in the collective memory of the country left by the *Gruendungsfieber* that preceded the crisis. One of the social phenomena engendered by the collapse of 1873 was the rise of Austrian anti-Semitism of which rather naturally the banks played an outstanding object.[13] But apart from the prolonged trauma inflicted by the bust of 1873, there were other, no less important factors involved. One surely was the long, highly unstable budgetary position of the state, which meant that the government's demand for assistance from the banks in its credit operations was deflecting the banks from industrial financing. In addition, forgetting the banks for a minute, there were both physical and man-made impediments to Austria's industrial development.[14]

[12] Cf. Carl Morawitz, *50 Jahre Geschichte*, p. 38.

[13] See the excellent study by Hans Rosenberg, *Grosse Depression und Bismarckzeit*, Berlin, 1967.

[14] Friedrich Hertz described them well in two studies: *Die Schwierigkeiten der industriellen Produktion in Oesterreich*, Vienna, 1913; and *Die Productionsgrundlagen der oesterreichischen Industrie vor und nach dem Kriege, insbesondere im Vergleich mit Deutschland*, Vienna-Berlin, s.a. (completed 1917).

Two: Economic Backwardness

The industrial centers of the country were far removed from the seas. The endowment of basic natural resources, except perhaps for magnesite, was a fraction of the resources Germany disposed of, and their dispersed location was an additional unfavorable factor. The main river of the "Danubian Monarchy" flowed through very undeveloped countries to a sea that was far removed from the busy ocean lanes. The strong position of the landed aristocracy in cabinets and civil service must also be mentioned in this connection. Members of the nobility did not mind participating personally on the boards of banking and industrial enterprises, but as public servants they were on the whole either wanting in interest or outright distrustful when industry was concerned. Finally, one must mention the discriminatory legislation, under the terms of which joint-stock companies were subject to special and extraordinarily high taxation. In these circumstances, one need not wonder why the German banks, in their so much more favorable environment, could pursue for several decades a policy that was much more innovative and aggressive than the comparatively more intermittent and more timid policies of the Austrian banks. How does all this relate to my approach and Rudolf's very restrained polemics against it?

Herbert Matis is inclined to think that the case of Austria supports my approach. After sketching a relevant portion thereof, he quotes Maerz's statement that "Austria's economic history is in large measure history of banks."[15] Flattering as Matis's rather cautiously stated endorsement is, I must decline the honor involved. Overlooked in assertions of this kind is the simple fact that the essence of my approach lies in an attempt to analyze what may be described as the natural history of great spurts of industrialization within the framework of nineteenth-century Europe. Nowhere did I claim that I regarded the great spurts as in any sense "inevitable." I spent a good deal of saliva and ink on trying to demonstrate that concepts of historical necessity or inevitability are destitute of meaning.[16]

[15] Herbert Matis, *Oesterreichs Wirtschaft*, pp. 164-165; and Maerz, *Oesterreichische Industrie- und Bankpolitik*, p. 11.

[16] Therefore if Cameron writes: "Gerschenkron has shown the fallacy of W. W. Rostow's concept of 'necessary prerequisites' or preconditions for industrialization, but by replacing prerequisites with 'substitutes' he comes dangerously close

Two: Economic Backwardness

In other words, my approach is entirely conditional or contingent. If *there occurred* a great spurt in conditions of medium economic backwardness in a European country that I have not yet studied, I should expect the banks to play a role as one element of the great spurt. This expectation may be verified or falsified as the case may be, but there is not a shred of "necessity" involved in the argument, which runs altogether in terms of probabilities and expectations. As I have often pointed out, the whole idea of substitutes may involve innovations, and what is truly "new" cannot be predicted in the very nature of novelty. Thus, it is possible that in a country, for reasons such as unfavorable attitudes toward banks and bankers, or inadequacy or insufficiency of talent in the banks, the activities of the banks in the great spurt may be supplemented by promotional activities of the state, despite the absence of an "extreme degree of backwardness." The function of an historical approach of this sort consists in establishing expectations that are turned into questions addressed to historical material, and the very failure of expectations to be redeemed may raise a number of further questions, productive of further research.

Nor did I ever deny that some industrialization can take place in advance of the great spurt as certainly was the case in Russia before the 1890s, or in Italy in the 1880s. What I do believe is that the discontinuity of the great spurt provides the basis for a sustained rate of industrial growth and for the reduction of the country's degree of economic backwardness. Now, there seems to be a general consensus, in which I join, that Austria never experienced a great spurt of modern industrialization in the nineteenth century. Both Richard Rudolf and David Good are in agreement on the subject. But if this be so, then Rudolf's fine article quite wrongly

---

to falling into the trap of 'historical inevitability,' " I must regard this statement as not only carelessly phrased ("dangerously close" indeed!) but entirely thoughtless and written in defiance of the author's own better knowledge. Professor Cameron may consider my concept of "substitution for missing prerequisites" as "most misleading." This is his good right, although, since no reasons for his belief are given, his assertion is little more than unadulterated abuse. In reality, my concept of substitutes has as little to do with any inevitabilities as Professor Cameron's statement with scholarly accuracy and straightforward thinking and writing. Cf. Rondo Cameron, ed., *Banking*, p. 12.

has been set up as a "test case" of an approach that is conditionally tied to the actual occurrence of a "great spurt." Accordingly, Rudolf conducts his polemics against a non-existing target. I doubt that he succeeds in reestablishing the absent target by splitting my argument, rather artificially I feel, into two parts and moving it to a question of fact, and claiming first that there was neither lack of entrepreneurial talent nor lack of availability of capital to private investors, nor, in fine, any "need" for large blocs of investment. In other words, that there was no "need" in Austria for a great spurt of industrialization. He proceeds to what he describes as the second part of my argument by making a distinction between "an expanded role of the banks" and seeing the banks "as engines of industrialization or as leaders in economic development." And he proceeds: "To begin with, one must ask why bankers, often characterized as a cautious breed, and wary of industrial investment to this day, should have been the initiators of industrialization in the mid-nineteenth century?"[17]

As far as the last question is concerned, I consider Rudolf's wonderings quite irrelevant in the light of what we know about the actual course of events in countries such as Germany and Italy. Can, for instance, Carl Fuerstenberg be characterized as "cautious breed" and a man wary of industrial investment? And how do Rudolf's lighthearted cogitations stand up against the fact that a generation later in the First Austrian Republic the banks controlled about 80 percent of total industrial capital? This fact does not seem to denote any "wariness of industrial investment." I might add that I have had a close personal opportunity of watching how, in the 1920s, the representatives of the *Credit Anstalt* appeared weekly at two machinery factories in a little industrial town near Vienna. They participated most intimately not just in all entrepreneurial, but in many managerial decisions, and their word was received as command by the directors of the two firms. In this sense, the limitations of Rudolf's horizon as a historian are rather disheartening. He did pay attention to the economic history of Imperial Austria, but seems to be blissfully unaware of the banking history either in Germany or in the Republic of Austria.

[17] Richard L. Rudolf, "Austria, 1800-1914," pp. 27-28.

More knowledge would have effectively prevented Rudolf from asking his inane rhetorical question.

As far as the first part of the argument goes, even Rudolf's mentor, Cameron, finds it difficult to reconcile the idea of capital abundance in Austria with the fact of strong foreign investment both in the public and the private sectors of the economy.[18] I believe that Rudolf has failed in his attempt to re-create the lost target. A priori psychologizing generalizations may help (if they are reasonable) to explain historical events, but they cannot erase them from the tablets of history. Nor can I consider well-founded the assertion that Austria had been developing just fine and accordingly did not "need" a great spurt. Quite apart from the mythical nature of the term "need," there remains the fact that in the last decades of the past century Austria slid more and more behind Germany, whose industry grew at a higher rate than that exhibited by Rudolf's index (whose degree of accuracy I am unable to judge), so that Austria's economic backwardness vis-à-vis Germany was increasing rather than decreasing.[19]

It is precisely Austria's failure to have had a great spurt of industrialization, the sluggishness of its growth, the weak cohesion of its provinces, and the glaring deficiencies in its system of communications that make me believe that, in the last years of the nineteenth century, Austria was ready for a great spurt of industrialization, or, in other and more personal terms, Austria was ready for Koerber.

But a related and pertinent question is: Was Koerber ready for Austria? The question has many implications. Was Koerber aware of how his plans related to the history of government-engineered spurts in Europe? Or, in other words, did Koerber's sight extend far enough beyond the boundaries of Austria, and how did his plans fit into the economic and spiritual environment of contemporaneous Europe, taking both the adjective and the noun in a very broad sense? There is no doubt that the higher rate of indus-

[18] Rondo Cameron, ed., *Banking*, p. 16.

[19] It ought to be worth mentioning in this connection that Maerz claims at the very end of his study that "on the eve of the First World War the Monarchy still was a large undeveloped area." Eduard Maerz, *Oesterreichische Industrie- und Bankpolitik*, p. 373.

trial growth in Germany was uppermost in Koerber's mind and perhaps was the main yardstick by which he gauged Austria's economic backwardness. In every respect—economically, socially, politically, culturally—Germany was, both from a general point of view and quite particularly from the point of view of a German civil servant in Austria, closer to the Austrian half of the Monarchy than any other country. It is, therefore, somewhat paradoxical that, while the German example stimulated imitation and emulation, Koerber's plans were "downright un-German" in terms of modern industrial history of Germany, where the role of the state in promoting industrial development had been clearly secondary.

Let us first view Koerber's plans in the light of relevant historical experience. In some sense, Koerber's ideas fitted well into the framework of the intellectual and economic history of the century that was drawing to its close at least by the yardstick of the calendar, although not by that of history. One aspect of Koerber's policy was to supplant nationalistic revolutions by industrial revolution. In other words, the economy was more important than politics. Was not just this the essence of the thought of the century as contained in both of its great intellectual movements— liberalism and socialism? Was not precisely this revealed by the Cobden-Chevalier treaty—the great and never forgotten triumph of free trade policies in the economic history of Europe, when a treaty of commerce became a treaty of peace and effectively eliminated the threat of war? Liberalism and socialism! Despite all the differences, very similar ideas were an integral part of the materialistic conception of history that had become the spiritual foundation of many labor movements, and especially of those in Central Europe. If the nineteenth century was the age of the primacy of the economic factor, what was more natural than an attempt to solve political difficulties by economic measures? Yet a simple formula of this sort does not necessarily do justice to the problems of a concrete case.

The point is that there was a good deal more to Koerber's ideas than the solution of a political problem. As will be shown later, the lack of appreciation of this simple point mars the discussion of the Koerber era both by the contemporaries and by historians.

They failed to understand that, in Koerber's plans, Austria's economic backwardness and the desire to reduce it had an importance of its own, quite independently of the political effects of the economic measures. Therefore, in addition to general intellectual affinities of Koerber's policy there is the problem of other cases of industrial spurts engineered and supported by the government and what Koerber had learnt, or should have learnt, from them.

Only two cases, of unequal relevance, come to mind, and should be discussed in the following: the case of France in the middle of the century and the case of Russia that immediately preceded the Koerber experiment. In the France of the early 1850s, Napoleon III tried to solve the perennial political problem of all modern dictatorship—its vindication—by concentrating on the economic development of the country and in the process having recourse both to the ideology of Saint-Simon and the energies and vitalities of the Saint-Simonians. As such it was still another case demonstrating the primacy of the economic factor to which I referred in the preceding paragraph. It will be useful to keep this historical precedent in mind, or rather to ask in what sense it was and in what sense it was not a precedent of Koerber's program and experiment.

The great spurt of economic development under the Second Empire proceeded indeed under the auspicious supervision and help of the government. But what the state contributed to the upsurge of economic energies was not a large investment program nor other measures of positive kind. The achievement of the government lay in the radical change of its foreign economic policy. By several acts that followed each other in quick succession, Napoleon III reduced the inordinately high import duties that did not protect but choked the country's economy and for decades had kept France in economic isolation from the world, and particularly from England. Thereby, the crucial retarding factor in French economic development was eliminated. For the rest, it was the credit mechanism—the new banks—that shouldered the task of economic growth. Thus, the direct action of the government was essentially negative and well in line with the laissez-faire ideas of the age, except, of course, that those ideas had been appropriated by, and built into the much more spacious and showy house of, the Saint-Simonian ideology. The feverish economic development in conjunction with that ideology was designed to provide the régime with the much needed raison d'être.

To mention these things is to indicate that, beyond one point of rather superficial resemblance, the setting within which Koerber found himself and to which his policies were adjusted was rather different. In both cases a political problem was to be solved by action in the economic sphere. But even the political problems, if not altogether different, were not really identical in the two cases. The years of internal discord had undermined the faith of the Austrians in their State. It had become fashionable to speak of the imminent disintegration of the Monarchy. To some extent, this was an old song. More than a quarter of the century before Koerber's advent to power, Karl Marx wrote to Engels from a vacation in Karlsbad: "The more details one hears about Austria, the more one is convinced that this State is on the way to its end."[20] The situation certainly had deteriorated enormously since Marx's writing in the early seventies. We know now, with the help of hindsight, that the process of disintegration should not have been exaggerated. Nearly a full decade after Koerber's resignation the allegedly disintegrating Monarchy was still able to live through four years of a disastrous and wholly unprecedented military effort. But to the eyes of the contemporaries, the situation at the end of the century looked grave indeed. In this sense, a vindication of the State was needed in Austria, as it had been in the Second Empire.

And yet, even in this respect the resemblance was far from perfect. Unlike Napoleon III, Francis Joseph was not a usurper, even though both monarchs came to the throne in the wake of simultaneous popular revolutions. Behind the Austrian Emperor stood nearly six centuries of dynastic history, and not, as in the case of Napoleon III, an alleged relationship to a great but dubious uncle. As a result, the Austrian *Obrigkeitsstaat* was a phenomenon very different from the Second Empire, which clearly was a modern dictatorship. An important consequence of this difference was that, for Napoleon III, the liberalization of the regime, when it

[20] Karl Marx–Friedrich Engels, *Briefwechsel*, Vol. IV, *1868-1883*, Berlin, 1950, p. 507.

came in the 1860s, while not necessarily adumbrating the speedy end of the dictatorship, was a clear sign of its diminished, if not waning power. By contrast, Francis Joseph could well accept some relaxation of pressures and rigidities of governmental practices and possibly even strengthen his rule in the process. And this was precisely one of the things Koerber tried to do and with a fairly lasting result. Thus, so far it seems that some more superficial resemblances and differences are tied together in a rather entangled skein.

But fundamental differences lay elsewhere. Koerber—the expert on tariff policies—was not a passionate free trader; nor was free trade, relations with Hungary apart, a crucial economic problem of the Monarchy.[21] Hence, quite unlike the French case, liberalization of foreign trade policies was not an obvious element of intensive policies of economic development. Moreover, the investment bank, the great innovation and the vehicle of economic progress in the Second Empire, had been established in Austria for many decades. For a number of previously mentioned reasons, the investment bank had made some intermittent rather than steady, and certainly no sensational contributions to the country's economic development. Thus the banks as such, in Koerber's thinking, were to have no more than subsidiary functions that had no bearing on the relations between banks and economic development. Therefore, the role that Koerber's program assigned to the state was not negative but very positive. The object was not removal by state action of impediments to development that had been created by previous actions of the state. The object was direct promotion of development by the state. As such, the policy intended to involve the Austrian government in matters of economic policies much more deeply than had been the case in

---

[21] The Austrian tariff, as it existed in the last decade of the nineteenth century, was protectionist indeed, but certainly not excessively so with its rates of customs duties between 15 and 30 percent *ad valorem*. See Johann von Bazant, *Die Handelspolitik Oesterreich-Ungarns*, Leipzig, 1894, p. 152. It may be in order to mention here my belief that, in European experience, protectionist tariffs in themselves did not lead to considerable accelerations of industrial growth. They could be helpful, if they were an integral part of broad measures designed to promote industrialization.

France. All this, however, does not mean that there was nothing for Koerber to learn from the French experience.

We will return to this question after a brief discussion of stimulations and lessons that could have been derived from the Russian experience. I have dealt elsewhere with the great spurt of industrial development in Russia and need not repeat myself here.[22] Only the salient parts needed for purposes of comparison should be mentioned. The general similarity is obvious. The Russian spurt, conducted under the overriding guidance of Count Witte (at that time not yet count), implied powerful investment of budgetary funds into economic development, centered to a large extent on the construction of railroads, although not confined to it. Here lies a certain resemblance between Witte and Koerber, because both men were concerned with railroad construction. But although Koerber had had close connection with the administration of Austrian railroads, his background in the area did not begin to approach Witte's, for whom railroads had constituted the origin and the basis of his remarkable career.

Overriding this resemblance was a crucial difference between the two men. As the engineer of Russia's policies of economic development, Witte was above all the powerful, resourceful, and inventive Minister of Finance. In this position, he could shape the revenues and the outlays of the country's budget in strict accordance with the needs of his economic plans and projects. He was able to increase the tax pressure on the peasantry to a sheerly intolerable height, and at the same time to cut from the budget expenditures that did not serve his economic plans. By contrast, Koerber, who in addition to being the Premier was also the Minister of the Interior and later even took over the Ministry of Justice, kept quite shy of the Ministry of Finance, for which he had invited Boehm-Bawerk, who as a civil servant was a stern man of rigid and unbending principles and great strength of character. During my perusal in the Austrian *Haus-, Hof-, und Staatsarchiv* of the meetings of the Common Council of Ministers, I was amazed at the boldness with which Boehm-Bawerk stood up against the financial wishes of the Emperor, who often presided over these

---

[22] Cf. Alexander Gerschenkron, *Economic Backwardness*, pp. 124 *et seq*.

meetings. No other minister ever tried to do that, everybody hastening in deeply ingrained servility to agree with the Emperor. But Boehm-Bawerk not only stood his ground but even went so far as to offer his resignation in the open meeting. Civil courage is a venerable quality. It happens, however, that there was not much to venerate about Boehm-Bawerk's role in our story. That Koerber was not his own Minister of Finance and that he had Boehm-Bawerk rather than somebody of more pliable nature in this position proved to be of decisive significance for the success or failure of the Koerber experiment. It will take me some time later in these lectures to provide literary and above all archival evidence in support of this statement.

It is in connection with the railroads that another element of difference must be mentioned. For Witte, economic development of Russia represented an intrinsic value as an engine of civilizing the most backward major country on the continent of Europe, a country to which Lenin frequently applied the adjective "savage" (*dikaya*). Koerber, too, often juxtaposed in his speeches "culture" and "economic progress." But in Russia the strategic significance of railroad construction was accepted as a matter of course. Witte had succeeded in impressing the idea firmly upon the slow and unsubtle but strong mind of his sovereign and patron, Alexander III. For some time at least the momentum of the parental tradition was operative with the son's (Nicholas II) hardly more subtle mind, but certainly weaker character. Witte understood well that some of the strategic railroads were a sacrifice from the point of view of speedy economic development, but regarded them as the price that inevitably had to be paid to secure support for his policy.

It was different in Austria. No one can read the previously mentioned minutes without being left with the impression that in the mind of Francis Joseph things military and things economic were lodged in two entirely separate compartments. His deep interest in the former was paralleled by lack of interest in, and understanding for, the latter. The old man knew how to insist vigorously on increasing the manpower of his army, but the relationship between the economic potential of the country and its military power appears to have lain outside his purview and concerns. This was strange enough, because Russia had been regarded for decades as

60

the most dangerous and dreaded enemy in a military conflict. Nevertheless, Francis Joseph seemed to be much more concerned with the Italian *irredenta* in Tyrol, even though Italy was an ally of the Monarchy. Perhaps the loss of Lombardy and Veneto still rankled in the Emperor's mind. At any rate, it seems fair to conclude that in Austria the policies of economic development lacked what in Russia had been one of their strongest supporting pillars. Curiously, it was only during World War I that the strategic significance of Koerber's main railroad became visible to everybody.

There was also something else. Russian public opinion had been concerned for a long time, but never so intensely as in the 1890s, with the problem of Russia's future, that is to say with the desirable (or predictable) direction of political, social, and economic development of the country. In this complex of problems (sometimes summarized in the question "Whither Russia?"), discussed with untiring persistence, considerable sophistication and erudition, and great passion, economic matters played a large and at times perhaps central part. The result was that within that curious group known as Russian intelligentsia there developed a body of thought and beliefs that can be properly described as an industrialization ideology. In the specific Russian conditions, that ideology, perhaps paradoxically and in all events surprisingly, took the form of Marxism. In Russian Marxism, the inevitability of industrialization (called capitalism) as demonstrated by "the last word of science" and the messianic promise of future bliss were inextricably conjoined. As such, they supplied approval of industrialization and justification of the manifold sacrifices and sufferings that its course entailed.

Koerber was a highly educated man; so was Sieghart, his main aide. There is, however, no evidence that Koerber ever was concerned with either the French experience of the 1850s or with that of Russia in the preceding decade. The fact is that when it comes to matters that go beyond Koerber's ideas of administrative reforms or his speeches and actions, we are rather poorly informed of the intellectual life of the man in general and his readings in particular.

Thomas Masaryk, the considerable scholar and the political leader of the Czechs in the Monarchy, as well as the first President of the Republic of Czechoslovakia, reporting on illuminating conversations with Koerber in the years of World War I, confidently stated that Koerber's memoirs "certainly will not get lost."[23] But Masaryk's expectation was deceived. Koerber left no memoirs. Their lack has been grievously felt throughout the work on these lectures. The memoirs would have enabled me to be much more definite in assessing Sieghart's contribution to Koerber's policies; and one must assume that they would have cast some light on Koerber's broad intellectual equipment with which he embarked upon his experiment.

We must, therefore, in summarizing the preceding pages, return to the question of what Koerber could or should have learnt from the cases of France and Russia. This is not idle speculation, because raising it should throw some light on Koerber's problems and prerequisites of success. Quite obviously the first thing that the knowledge of the Russian spurt would have told him would have been to suggest that his plans presupposed in one form or the other the mastery over the Ministry of Finance. In saying this one has, of course, to keep in mind that a finance minister in absolutist Russia naturally had an infinitely wider range of action than his counterpart in the constitutional Monarchy of Austria. Yet understanding that by no means eliminates the problem.

Moreover, a study of these two cases would have convinced Koerber that a fixed industrialization program may require the support of an ideology that introduces into the body social far-flying ideas that add to the material benefits something that ignites the imagination of men. The Saint-Simonians were not simply establishing a new bank; they also claimed to be building "a new heaven and a new earth" and laying the basis for the golden age that lay in front of mankind. The Russian Marxians felt themselves to be executors of "the orders of history," acting in fulfillment of its immutable laws, and in addition preparing the ineluctable advent of the just and good order of socialism.

Whether or not Koerber was aware of these precedents, he understood that his program, to put it crudely, must be "sold" to people. Hence his numerous speeches and his use of the press.

[23] Thomas G. Masaryk, *The Making of a State*, New York, 1927, p. 26.

Two: Economic Backwardness

His speeches appealed to material interests and as such were not unpersuasive, but probably not what the moment was calling for. In this connection, it is illuminating to read of Koerber's consultations with Theodor Herzl. Herzl, the agitator and propagandist of genius, knew in his bones what was required. In discussing with Koerber a speech that the premier was preparing, Herzl kept urging the need "to be popular," "to appeal to imagination" and in general "to the population over the heads of professional politicians," using "new meaningful slogans." Herzl offered to prepare for Koerber a *"sursum corda"* appeal, as he said, to be addressed manifesto-like to the peoples of Austria. And when Koerber recited to Herzl in advance of delivery one of his much admired oratorical performances, Herzl knew at once what was wrong with it: "The speech is too bureaucratic, Excellency. The tone of a proclamation is missing." Interestingly enough, in view of what has been said before about the authorship of Koerber's speeches, the Premier once had indeed asked Herzl to draft a speech for him, but then to Herzl's dismay gave an entirely different speech.[24]

One can only conclude that it was not given to Koerber, the civil servant, to act as a popular tribune, and to imitate men like Danton or Bebel and, according to a line of Pushkin's, "to inflame men's hearts by the word." In Vienna at that time only Karl Lueger, the Mayor of the City, knew how to do such things with immense success, but Koerber probably had a good deal of contempt for the great demagogue, from whom Hitler had learned so much. It must also be considered that confecting an ideology to order or finding one to rely on was not exactly easy in Austria of the period. In Germany, after the brief flurry of Saint-Simonian influence, it was nationalism that for some time greased the wheels of German industrialization before they started turning so very fast and no longer needed any ideological acceleration.

Obviously, in Austria nationalism was a divisive rather than cohesive force, as there were altogether too many "nationalisms" at loggerheads with each other. It was therefore patriotism, not nationalism, that Koerber could appeal to and, in fact, did in his

[24] Theodor Herzl, *Tagebuecher*, Vol. II, pp. 417-418, 442-443.

many references to the interests of the state and his stress on the benefits to be derived from a large unified area, to which his policies were clearly hitched. But patriotism as an ideology? A couple of decades earlier Eduard Bernstein, a sharp observer and a keen mind, wrote to Engels: "I have met Austrians of all parties, but all those with whom I spoke had one point in common, their lack of patriotism."[25] During the twenty years that had elapsed since the 1880s, things probably deteriorated rather than improved in this aspect. Yet, it would be certainly wrong to assume that Austrian patriotism was altogether non-existent. When the First World War broke out, Sigmund Freud, a man not given to entertaining conventional opinions, pronounced that "all his libido" was attached to the Monarchy. And, as said before, there came in the following years "mass confirmations" of that individual statement. Nevertheless the main point remains: whatever the strength of Austrian patriotism, an ideology cut out of it could not possibly approach in strength of texture an ideology made of nationalism in Germany.

But what has been said so far does not at all exhaust the problem of why Koerber did not offer an ideology that could have served as a flying banner for his policies. But after all, Witte did not offer such an ideology either, because Witte's interest in Friedrich List was essentially confined to the approval of the infant industry argument (which he faithfully passed on in his lectures to the Crown Prince, the future Nicholas II), but List's combination of mild Saint-Simonianism and strong nationalism was not what Witte preached. The "industrialization ideology" came, as it were, from outside, as far as Witte was concerned. Could a replica be found in Austria?

In asking this question we must return once more to the previously touched upon problem of the attitude toward Koerber of the Austrian Social-Democratic party. Koerber was indeed a godsend for the party. For years the press organ of the Social Democrats had carried a column "How we are treated," which became celebrated in the history of the Austrian labor movement. It was a daily column, and nearly every day supplied fresh material for it.

[25] Cf. Helmut Hirsch, ed., *Eduard Bernsteins Briefwechsel mit Friedrich Engels*, Assen, 1970, p. 76 (February 17, 1882).

Two: Economic Backwardness

The fundamental civil rights laid down in the constitution of 1867 were regularly disregarded when workers and their party were involved. The state prosecutors could confiscate in the press anything they pleased without approval by the courts. After the event, confiscations could be appealed, but the government could rely on its judges to reject the appeals, and the only purpose of the appeals was to bring the matter to the knowledge of the public. The arbitrary decision, or rather whim, of an uneducated police representative could dissolve any meeting at any time because of "criticism of authorities." In addition to its chapters "Freedom of the Press" and "Freedom of Assembly," the column also included the chapters on "Freedom of Association" and "Freedom of Coalition." Moreover, the socialist editors and speakers were regularly indicted on the basis of antiquated and elastic articles of the penal code and sentenced to both fines and arrests.

In the 1890s, Victor Adler, the venerated leader and, in fact, creator of the party, spent some time in jail nearly every year. The extremely busy, overworked man used these periods for the study of Marxism and the first time even received from Engels a detailed set of directions regarding the most efficient way of absorbing Volume II and III of *Das Kapital*. Subsequently the Austrian courts did not fail to provide the opportunities for further study of Marx's work. And in addition to police, state prosecutors, and judges, there were the district chiefs (*Bezirkshauptleute*) who were very frequently youngish men of noble descent. After they had received their law degree, they were sent out as local chiefs of the government administration equipped with enormous power, ruling in inapproachable pride, and ever-ready to side against labor in any wage conflict, calling out the military on the slightest provocation and deciding against individual laborers in every recourse of individuals to administration. That column (How We Are Being Treated) in the Viennese *Arbeiter Zeitung* untiringly presented the facts on all those discriminatory policies, with their bending and breaching of the law, and performed a great job of education of public opinion. There is no doubt that Koerber had been very familiar with the column.

Nor is there any doubt that Koerber as Prime Minister changed all that. He was and wanted to be a "modern man." As such, he went on to "modernize" the administration of both the Ministries of the Interior and Justice.[26] He instructed the state prosecutors to stop their confiscating practices. He even submitted to the Parliament a bill containing a "modern press law."[27] And Koerber changed the social composition of the group of district chiefs by appointing many more commoners and more mature and experienced civil servants to those positions, and issuing a number of decrees instructing those civil servants to pay close attention to the needs of the population and to be fully accessible to the petitioners and the plaintiffs.

Were the Social Democrats appreciative of the great change that Koerber had wrought for them? Privately, Victor Adler knew very well how Koerber had affected Adler's own life. In 1903, he wrote to Karl Kautsky humorously: "Koerber ruins us, and particularly me intellectually, because he does not put us in jail any more."[28] More than a year later (December 9, 1904), when Vienna was full of rumors concerning Koerber's impending resignation, Adler wrote to the same correspondent regarding Marx's *Theories of Surplus Value*: "I shall be able to read them only if Koerber has really fallen today. Then comes a reactionary ministry [providing] jail and an opportunity to read. But unfortunately, it is not certain that Koerber will actually go in order to promote our scholarly education."[29]

At the party congress in the Fall of 1904, when Koerber's position was extremely shaky, Adler recited a somewhat premature farewell to the Premier that was not humorous at all and very re-

[26] It is with considerable reluctance that I use words such as "modern" or "modernizing," even though the terms were in much use at the time. But I find the use of the term "modernization" to replace "industrialization" or "industrial or economic development" highly misleading and problematic. There will be a later opportunity in these lectures to discuss this particular matter.

[27] In this he was less successful. Under the old press law even the vending of newspapers in the streets was forbidden, and the prohibition remained in force. When the First World War broke out in 1914 and the government could no longer prohibit the sale in the streets of all those special editions *(Extraausgaben)* announcing events on the battlefields, those editions were made subject to a specially introduced tax.

[28] Victor Adler, *Briefwechsel mit August Bebel und Karl Kautsky*, Vienna, 1954, p. 413.

[29] *Ibid.*, p. 440.

strained in tone: "Herr von Koerber is content to be the last bureaucrat who provides a decent exitus to the rule of bureaucracy in Austria. A decent exitus, that we cannot deny because some changes in the administrative practice have in fact occurred, changes which we had demanded as necessary for a very long time. Koerber recognized that these reforms had been overdue. I do not deny . . . that we enjoy today a much greater measure of freedom of the press, [more] perhaps than Austria ever possessed; [and] that our administrative authorities are instructed to respect more than before our freedom of association and assembly." This praise, phrased and pressed forth with such an obvious reluctance, was followed by even less complimentary remarks: "Herr von Koerber may glorify in the little changes which he has introduced. Nevertheless, just as were his predecessors, he is a man of retrogression, a man of Austrian halfheartedness, a man of criminal weakness."[30] Three years later, with Koerber gone about as long, Adler still spoke in a similar vein to the party congress of 1907: "Nor do we have any reason to speak a word of thanks to these Ministers, above all to Koerber who introduced that change of the [administrative] practice. We owe them no more than the recognition that they did what they had been forced to regard as necessary by the political work of Social Democracy."[31]

One will understand that it was difficult for leaders of a party that clung to a revolutionary ideology to go overboard in the public praise of a Habsburg minister. But they had every reason to be beholden to a man who had done away with ruthless discrimination practiced against the movement and had established a tradition of liberal policy which, as the last quotation shows, even his successors could not help continuing. It was also natural for Social Democracy, as it would be for any political party confronted with the job of agitation, to emphasize its own contribution to the progress that had been attained. Distance had to be kept. Yet, when everything is said and done, the fact remains that, in the whole history of Austria from 1867 to 1900, Cisleithania had no chief of the government who was in the least friendly to the labor movement and understanding of its problems.

[30] Victor Adler, *Aufsaetze, Reden, Briefe*, Vol. VIII, p. 247.
[31] *Ibid.*, p. 292.

Two: Economic Backwardness

It is precisely in view of these circumstances that our main problem must be posed. Politics apart, why did Social Democracy fail to provide strong ideological support, in fact an ideology, for a man whose main political idea was so much in line both with the ideology of the party and with what surely were its own interests. The extreme nationalisms threatened the cohesion and the normal operation of the Austrian state. But as the future would shortly show, they were also threatening the unity and cohesion of the labor movement itself.

On the other hand, economic development and industrialization were the fulfillment of Marxian "inevitables" from which the organized labor movement emerged. Whatever one might think of Marx's predictions in general, the foretold transformation of a "class in itself" into a class "for itself" doubtlessly did occur on a most impressive scale. Every new railroad, every new factory, every promotion of industrialization meant nearly automatic increases of the membership of the Social Democratic party. As will be remembered, Engels had urged this elementary point upon Victor Adler. It would have been natural, therefore, for Social Democracy to place its very considerable intellectual strength and its powerful machinery of agitation at the service of Koerber's plans. It would not have been difficult for the socialist pens to present Koerber as the engine of great historical change and to draw on the dubious but effective Marxian deterministic vocabulary to demonstrate or at least to argue the extreme futility of opposing ineluctable social forces. Yet not a single significant article, let alone a book, dealing with Austrian economic backwardness and the ways of overcoming it came from those quarters.

Moreover, Koerber may not have known much about Russian debates, but Austrian Social Democrats had many personal and other contacts with Russian Socialists, whom they met at the meetings of the Second International and whose polemics very often spilled over onto the pages of the Social Democratic newspapers and journals in Germany. And Russia was near to Austria in many respects. Less than one year after Koerber's resignation, the outburst of the First Revolution in Russia gave the most powerful impetus for the initiation of the final Austrian struggle for the general franchise. Granting that political history is likely to be

68

much more influential than intellectual history, the complete void of influence in this case is nevertheless quite surprising.

Hans Mommsen has written a voluminous book on Social Democracy and the problem of nationalities in the Habsburg's multinational state.[32] This book, distinguished more by the author's industry than wealth of ideas, devotes a couple of dozen pages to the Koerber era. Unlike the rest of the book, those pages are superficial, not overly accurate factually, and contain rather glib generalizations. Thus Mommsen speaks of the "optimistic expectations" with which the socialists were filled by Koerber's advent to power, which hopes were quickly deceived.[33] No reference is given for these statements, which are clearly at variance with Adler's remarks in 1900. Much of Mommsen's stricture of Koerber repeats the superficialities in the literature on Koerber, to which I shall return later on. Mommsen's statement that "Social Democracy had rushed into parliamentary activity because it believed that it was the easiest to obtain political success there" coupled with the remark "that this proved to be an error,"[34] shows more than anything else a propensity to judge rashly. When Mommsen interprets Adler's speech about Koerber to the party congress in 1903 by saying: "Adler's skepticism derived not in the last instance from the *very painful experience* which the Social Democrats had to undergo under the Koerber government," this assertion defies comprehension.[35] Note in addition that the statement ignores the problem of the missed opportunities in 1902 about which much will have to be said somewhat later. Mommsen is right, of course, in saying that "Koerber's intention to place the economic problems into the foreground as against national problems was in accordance with the line of the Party,"[36] but he does not see at all the ideological consequences of this obvious statement, and thus misses the historical problem that has preoccupied us in the last few paragraphs.

[32] Hans Mommsen, *Die Sozialdemokratie und die Nationalitaetenfrage im habsburgischen Vielvoelkerstaat*, Vienna, 1963, Vol. I.

[33] *Ibid.*, pp. 342-343.

[34] *Ibid.*, p. 346.

[35] *Ibid.*, p. 350. Italics supplied.

[36] *Ibid.*, p. 342.

Two: Economic Backwardness

There are a number of things one could mention when wondering about the Social Democrats' so-called failure to support Koerber in the way indicated. Perhaps one does not have to probe very deeply in searching for the reasons. Possibly, lack of imagination provides an intellectually dissatisfying, but nevertheless correct, explanation. Possibly, Engels's absence from the scene explains something. In the light of Engels's views on the subject of industrialization, one may assume that Koerber's program would have appealed to him. In all probability, he would have advised the Austrians who were ever-ready to listen to the voice of the master to make a great *Tamtam* in support of Koerber, as the old man Engels might have said in his amusing style that never quite shed the student slang of his youth. But Engels had been dead for a lustrum by the time Koerber first unveiled his program. On the other hand, it is possible that the socialists' sights in Austria were too closely riveted to Germany, where industrialization proceeded without the need of ideological support. Finally, while Austria was backward enough to need Koerber, it was not backward enough to have an intelligentsia as the Russian, which, insulated from action, devoted itself entirely to speculative thought. At any rate, whatever the reason, the fact remains that the Social Democracy, or rather the Austrian Marxism, left Koerber in the lurch, and the Koerber experiment had to proceed without the prop of an effective and captivating ideology.

And that was precisely what Koerber did. As soon as the newly elected Parliament convened and the forthcoming investment bills were discussed between the government and the representatives of the political parties, it appeared that a new wind was blowing through the corridors of the Second Chamber. Indeed, the Czechs proved willing to let the law concerning recruits for the army pass without obstruction. It seems, however, that at that point Koerber did not yet trust the improvement in the parliamentary situation to be more than quite temporary. Early in March 1901 he addressed the First Chamber (*Herrenhaus*), and there, after the earnest admonition concerning the urgent need of productive parliamentary labor, he offered a thinly veiled threat of a coup d'état. Without using the term, he said that in certain circumstances the emergency legislation (under article 14) might be insufficient and

70

a "bold grasp" (*kuehner Griff*) reaching more deeply might become necessary and excusable because provoked by the conditions in Parliament. It seems, however, that the threat produced much less impression on the public than a little phrase Koerber used to characterize the main tenor of the policies he intended to pursue. He said: "I can work no miracles. I have only one medicine in my little chest (*Hausmittel*), and that is *passionless perseverance (leidenschaftslose Beharrlichkeit)*."[37] The phrase remained memorable. It was much quoted and readily used and re-used by the Prime Minister himself. It was precisely one of those felicitous expressions that contributed so much to Koerber's reputation as an orator.

No miracles? And yet, as though to give the lie to Koerber's statement, a miracle did take place. On June 1, 1901, the Second Chamber voted not only without any obstruction but in an atmosphere of considerable enthusiasm two investment bills: one regarding construction of railroads and another regarding inland waterways (canals and river regulations). After adoption by the First Chamber and after having received the Emperor's sanction, the two laws appeared on the Statute Book as acts of June 11, 1901.

The two acts envisaged an investment by the government, roughly in equal parts in the two areas of construction, of one billion crowns. The figure impressed itself on the mind of the public within and without the Parliament, and men spoke excitedly of the "gold rain" with which the economy of the country was being showered. Now, how much was one billion crowns at that time? Converted at mint par, it amounted to a bit more than 200 millions of contemporary dollars. Converted at purchasing power, a somewhat higher amount would be likely to result. But such conversions do not mean much, and comparisons to contemporary Austrian magnitudes would be more enlightening. Total share capital invested at that time in Austrian banks amounted to 777 million crowns.[38] The total budget of the Austrian state for 1901 as submitted by Boehm-Bawerk to the Second Chamber,

[37] *Stenographisches Protokoll, Herrenhaus*, Session XVII, Meeting 4, March 2, 1901, p. 45. Italics supplied.

[38] Cf. Rudolf, "Austria, 1800-1914," p. 49.

amounted to roughly 1.6 billion crowns.[39] It is almost impossible
to say what the annual value added by industry was at the time. A
very hazardous computation leads me to believe that it may have
been somewhere between 2.25 and 2.5 billion crowns.[40]

So seen, the amount of one billion crowns appears to have been
quite considerable, apart from the verbal mystique involved in the
word *Milliarde*, two decades before the term was dwarfed by the
run-away inflations after World War I. But the appearance was
deceptive, particularly in comparisons with annual data. For the
billion begins to shrink rapidly once it is considered that the railroad construction took up to five (and in one case eight) years and
the construction of waterways extended for 20 years. The years
before 1904 were to be filled with preliminary studies, and the
government was empowered by the act to spend until 1912 the
maximum of 250 million crowns (not counting, however, the contributions to canals by the provinces and private interest), for
which amount bonds bearing 4-percent interest were to be issued.

The historical appraisal of the significance of the figure proposed must needs be judged in psychological and speculative
terms. For one, it certainly represented a *novum* for the period. So
far, the movement away from the liberal doctrines since the crisis
of 1873 essentially consisted in measures of social policy, mostly
designed to counteract the rising labor movement, and in measures aiming to help the small artisan and shopkeeper. But here the
purpose was to mobilize the state in order to start a big industrial
upsurge that could not but result in favoring modern industry and
in enlarging the share of industrial labor in the population. Possibly then, the two bills in conjunction with the rebuilding of the
port of Triest and a general bill of measures to facilitate the operations of industrial enterprises were laying the basis for a new tradition for the role of the state in its relation to the economic devel-

[39] Gustav Kolmer, *Parlament und Verfassung*, Vol. VIII, p. 185; Eugen Lopus-
zanski, *Die Volkswirtschaft Oesterreichs in den Jahren 1900 bis 1904*, Vienna,
1904, p. 64.

[40] Calculated highly uncertainly from data in Nachum Theodor Gross, "Industrialization in Austria in the Nineteenth Century," Ph.D. Dissertation, University
of California, Berkeley, 1954, p. 181, in conjunction with the previously mentioned index of industrial output by Rudolf, "Austria, 1800-1914," p. 20. The
purpose here is, of course, just to give an idea of the possible order of magnitude.

opment of the country. It is from this point of view that the significance of the amount of money should be considered. As a *first step* to be followed in reasonably quick succession by other like-minded measures, the figure was far from being negligible. Everything then depended on the *next steps*, and this is indeed crucial for a general evaluation of the Koerber program. Around this point were to turn its success and failure.

Before concluding this lecture, something more must be said on the following subjects: 1) More details on railroad construction and some of its geographic and technical problems; 2) an elucidation of the contents of the bill concerning the inland waterways; 3) an explanation of how Koerber's economic bills succeeded in laying the ghost of obstruction; and 4) Koerber's rise to the height of success in the summer of 1902, when the scale of destiny—his own and possibly that of the Monarchy—began to oscillate in his hands.

The railroad bill passed in 1901 was identical with that submitted in 1900, to which reference was made in Lecture One. The need to take care of the neglected "periphery" of the country was strong upon Koerber's mind. Hence the bill included construction of a line from Lemberg (the capital of the province of Galicia) to the Carpathian Mountains; and in the far South-West a connection between Dalmatia and the (then) occupied (and not yet annexed) provinces of Bosnia-Herzegovina; projects of that kind were stubbornly and narrow-mindedly fought by Hungary, which feared any increase in Austria's influence in the occupied provinces. Apart from other smaller railroads, the *pièce de résistance* of the whole plan was no doubt the Tauern-Karawanken railroad, designed to provide the second connection by rail to Triest. The relatively short Pyhrn Pass railroad was to provide the shortest connection between Prague, as the capital of Bohemia, and Triest. The two railroads (see map) were therefore parts of one system. The new railroad would both enhance the economic possibilities of Triest *and* increase the claims upon the port.[41] Thus the projected simultaneous expansion of the port shows the breadth of

[41] The port of Triest had gone through years of relative stagnation when the expansion of its facilities provided by the municipality of Triest had proved quite inadequate. See Johann von Bazant, *Die Handelspolitik*, pp. 76-78.

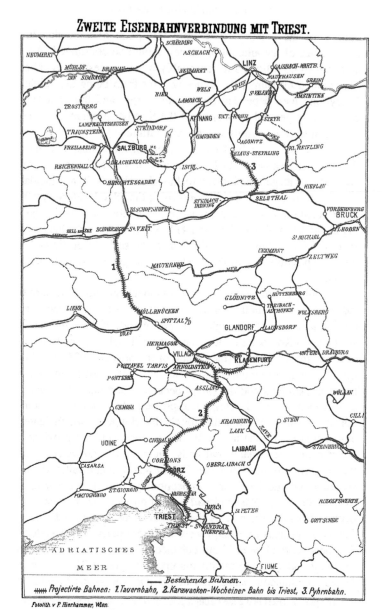

Koerber's Second Railroad to Trieste

74

Koerber's sights. In the process of preparing the bill, many an old problem had to be brushed aside or reasonable solutions found. Thus the old conflict between the Carinthian towns of Klagenfurt and Villach was solved by constructing a new line connecting Klagenfurt with the Karawanken railroad (see the map). The Predil railroad had been long under discussion, would have been an alternative to the Karawanken railroad, and would have been preferable both from the engineering and the economic points of view, but was abandoned "in the general interest of the State,"[42] as the government report somewhat cryptically said. But one can assume that this decision was based on Koerber's political decision to let the railroad go through Carniola and thus arouse the Slovenians' interest in the project. Indeed, during the parliamentary debates in 1901, a Slovenian deputy (Ferjančič) welcomed the decision, because the Predil railroad would have avoided Carniola.[43] It should be in order to interject here that because Carniola was Cisleithanian Koerber could do something for the Slovenians, while the fact that Croatia was a part of Transleithania severely retrenched the territorial amplitude for the application of Koerber's ideas.

Looking now at the technology of the projected railroad, one cannot but marvel at the boldness of the decision. In planning the crossing of the central crest of the Alps, no less than six or seven alternatives had been discussed. The Tauern railroad chosen no doubt provided the shortest and quickest connection with Triest. It involved the construction of a tunnel 8.6 kilometers long through the extremely hard gneiss granite of the crest at an altitude of more than 1,200 meters. The hardness of the rock rapidly wore out drilling machines and tools, the acquisition of which must be regarded as a backward linkage of the railroads along with the forward linkage involved in the need to produce additional engines and rolling stock to operate on the new railroads. The nature of the work was not the only difficulty to overcome. The work in the tunnel encountered what the Austrians

[42] *Stenographisches Protokoll, Haus der Abgeordneten,* Beilagen, Session XVI, Nr. 485, p. 17.

[43] *Stenographisches Protokoll, Haus der Abgeordneten,* Session XVII, Meeting 50 (May 23, 1901), p. 4200. See later Kramář's reference to Carniola.

called "knallendes Gebirge" (explosive Mountain). Avalanches, which created a number of catastrophes, necessitated protective constructions up the mountainside. Tourists comfortably crossing the Tauern on their way from Salzburg to the warm lakes of Carinthia or to Venice ought to think of the anonymous heroes who lost life and limb fighting the Alpine rock.

The Karawanken tunnel of 8,000 meters was drilled through much softer limestone, but there "rock deformations," water, and gas combined to make the work particularly hazardous. The manifold problems of accesses to the tunnels along the mountainsides involving many bridges and viaducts as well as the number of shorter tunnels and the difficulties presented by the bare "Karst" landscape south of the Alps may go unmentioned. By contrast, it may be said that the two main tunnels were constructed by what has come to be called the "Austrian Method," that is to say, simultaneous drilling in two stories with breaking through the floor or ceiling every 100 meters and thus opening the whole profile. The method is said to have been widely imitated in constructing mountain railways beyond the borders of Austria.[44]

It is unfortunately in the very nature of the waterways project that it cannot be discussed in any fashion comparable to that of the railroads. For what can be described are the plans rather than their execution. While the main thrust of the Railroad Bill pointed southward to the Adriatic Sea, the main thrust of the Waterways Bill pointed north, and beyond the borders of Austria to the Baltic Sea and the North Sea. Article One of the bill stipulated following navigable constructions: (1) a canal from the Danube to the Oder; (2) a canal from the Danube to Moldau (Vltava) near Budweis as well as the canalization of the Moldau from Budweis to Prague; (3) a canal from the Donau-Oder Canal to the middle reaches of the Elbe River as well as canalization of a stretch of the Elbe River; and, finally, (4) a connection between the Danube-Oder Canal to the Vistula Basin and to a navigable stretch of the Dniester River. In addition, Article Five of the bill provided for regulation of rivers in Bohemia, Moravia, Silesia, Galicia, as well as in

---

[44] For the preceding, see Aloys von Czedik, *Die Entwicklung der oesterreichischen Eisenbahnen als Privat- und Staatsbahnen, 1824-1910*, Teschen-Vienna-Leipzig, 1913.

Lower and Upper Austria.[45] From Koerber's vague introductory remarks in 1900, he had traveled a long way to the present act in which those remarks appear amplified and engraved in the proper juridical language upon the statute book. And yet, in another sense the road should have been a good deal longer, and the act better prepared than it actually was.

The central piece of the legislation was no doubt the Danube-Oder Canal. The construction of such a canal was considered as early as the seventeenth century. The mercantilists were outstanding as canal builders, and so it is not surprising that both Maria Theresa and Joseph II devoted attention to canals.[46] In 1872 the government submitted to Parliament a bill to build a canal connecting the Danube and the Oder. The bill, based on a project prepared by the Anglo-Bank, was accepted by both houses of the Parliament, but its execution fell victim to the crisis of 1873.[47]

The scheme, as presented in the 1901 act, reveals the grandeur of the view of its creators. Its potential economic significance was no doubt great. The bulky products of the North, particularly coal, could be moved cheaply southward to the industries of Vienna and Lower Austria and brought in the vicinity of the Styrian iron industry. Austria would become connected with the huge port of Hamburg, and products of Austrian industry could reach the industrial buyers in Saint Petersburg by water. A basic disability of Austria's economic geography would have been removed, and one could reasonably expect that new industries would come to settle along the banks of the new waterways. With ideology or without ideology, the project was something to ignite imagination.

And it did ignite the imagination. The bills proved irresistible. On the left wing of the Social Democratic party there was some opposition in principle to Koerber, and one of the leaders of that wing, Winarsky, tried to voice it at the party congress of 1901

[45] Act of June 11, 1901, *Reichsgesetzblatt* 66 of June 13, 1901. See Appendix 1.

[46] Particularly, it seems, to a connection between the Danube and the Elbe Rivers. Cf. Gustav Otruba, *Die Wirtschaftspolitik Maria Theresias*, Vienna, 1963, pp. 159-160.

[47] See Carl Morawitz, *50 Jahre Geschichte*, pp. 29-30; and Ferdinand Lettmayer, ed., *Wien um die Mitte des XX Jahrhunderts*, Vienna, 1958, p. 83.

after Koerber's bills had been voted upon. But Victor Adler silenced him effectively. He said: "Winarsky says: That man Koerber has a devilish plan. He wants to play his economics against our politics. . . . The faction (he says) has committed the crime of supporting Koerber's policy by omission and approval. . . . Does Winarsky believe that it would have been a very intelligent policy on the part of our fraction and would have been in the interest of the working class for us to have voted against the canals? I am not of that opinion."[48] Note that Victor Adler did not use this opportunity to elaborate on the significance of Koerber's economic development plans for the Austrian working class. He took the matter for granted and did not say a word more than was needed to brush Winarsky aside.

But it was not the social revolutionaries that constituted a problem. It was the nationalist revolutionaries, first and foremost the Czechs, and then the Slovenians, whose obstruction had paralyzed the Parliament. As Lecture One indicated, the Czechs received Koerber's economic program in 1900 with rejection and mockery. The Railroad Bill, despite the Pyhrn Pass project, was regarded as something of profit only to the German Alpine provinces. In this respect, too, the Czech minds had been disabused. Several years later, in re-thinking and re-discussing the events of the period, Karel Kramář, the leader of Czech radicalism, had to admit: "Dr. von Koerber tried to extinguish the fire of our obstruction by the gold rain of a few hundreds millions to be used for investments. Besides, by his bill regarding the Alpine railroads, he had won the Slovenians, our closest allies, and the Slovenians in turn influenced us by using the weighty argument of their economic needs."[49] This shows that Koerber's decision to let the railroad pass through Carniola had the desired effect not only upon the Slovenians, but also upon the Czechs.

The Canal Bill was introduced by Koerber on April 26, 1901, in a quiet and dignified speech. He described the contents of the bill, spoke of the technical difficulties of constructing canals in a mountainous country where the canals had to overcome very considerable differences in altitude and intimated that just as Austria

[48] Victor Adler, *Aufsaetze, Reden, Briefe*, Vol. VIII, p. 216.
[49] Karel Kramář, *Anmerkungen*, p. 50.

has been trailblazing in railroad construction through mountains, he hoped it would perform the same function in canals. He mentioned that geography entailed both high cost of construction and high cost of operation for the canals, and added that therefore there was no certainty that the revenues would cover interest and amortization and the canals might even be run at a loss. Was it wise to make such statements at that point? But Koerber was not a demagogue; a serious and honest man, he tried to impress upon the Parliament that what mattered was not the narrow concept of profitability, but the broad concept of advantages to accrue to the national economy. This, he was sure, was understood by the population of the relevant provinces, which for decades had been clamoring for canals. He finished by saying that it would scarcely have been possible to submit to the house a more important and more meaningful bill.

Two more points remain to be made with regard to Koerber's speech. He referred specifically to the last article of the bill (Article 17 in the finally adopted version), which read: "The execution of this act is entrusted to the cabinet as a whole (*das Gesamtministerium*)." The Prime Minister then said: "This does not mean merely that almost all the ministries will participate in administering this act, but that the government is conscious both of the significance of the matter and of the seriousness of the situation. What we are about to undertake is an altogether novel task for Austria." We shall see later how faithfully at least one of the members of the Cabinet executed the trust he had accepted by placing his signature upon the act, and we must wonder whether some premonitions made Koerber include Article 17 in the bill and go out of his way to emphasize its importance.

The second point because of which we actually retraced our steps to return to the introduction of the bill by the Prime Minister is this: one scans that introductory speech in vain in search of some reference to river regulations. There was none. And what is more, there was none in the bill.[50] The failure to include river

[50] For Koerber's speech, see *Stenographisches Protokoll, Haus der Abgeordneten*, Session XVII, Meeting 37 (April 26, 1901), pp. 2896-2897. The Danube-Oder Canal was supposed to overcome altitudes between 100 and 288 meters and a Danube-Elbe connection altitudes between 216 and 417 meters. See *Steno-*

regulations in the bill was all the stranger as Koerber had induced the Emperor to include in the throne speech of February 4, 1901, a reference to floods that had occurred and the consequent "duty of my government" to carry through river regulations.[51] But Koerber apparently wanted to keep the Canal Bill simple and was unwilling to increase its costs and perhaps fearful to do so. We shall see why.

This, however, changed drastically as soon as the bill was sent into the committee. There not only was it received with enthusiasm but the committee began urging the government to expand the bill by including river regulations, and in these urgings no one could equal the eagerness of the Czech deputies, who only a year earlier had taken such a dismal view of Koerber's program. The result was that the bill emerged from the committee in a greatly expanded shape. When the whole house convened to debate the bill, the first thing that the *rapporteur*, the deputy Max Menger, stressed was the great change between the original bill and the bill that eventually came to the house. It should be noted that not only the bill had altered, but that also Max Menger, the brother of Carl and Anton, the two professors referred to before, had changed his views. In 1900, Max Menger, the Liberal deputy, mainly expressed his reservations vis-à-vis government investment and enterprises run by bureaucracy. Not a shadow of those reservations was in evidence now, and Menger was the main official advocate of the bill before the Parliament. He emphasized the need for speed in passing the bill, because the Hungarians had also been considering a plan for a Danube-Oder Canal that would, by using the Waag River, by-pass Cisleithania and deprive the latter of its advantages. Thus, there was a clear *periculum in mora*. In discussing those advantages to Austria, Menger's praise had few limits. *Inter alia*, he argued that the canals would stop the emigration from Cisleithania to overseas, which had been draining the country of its labor power. With considerable gusto, Menger calculated the total cost of river regulations (which was to be additional to the original bill) and arrived

---

graphisches Protokoll, Haus der Abgeordneten, Beilagen, Session XVII, Nr. 792, p. 12.

[51] Gustav Kolmer, *Parlament und Verfassung*, Vol. VIII, p. 147.

for the next twelve years at the sizable figure of 300-400 million crowns (including in it the contributions of the provinces).[52]

The debate that followed was not without voices of dissent. The canals were opposed by the agrarian interests, that is to say, by the peasants under the leadership of the "feudal" large estate owners. They claimed that the canals in the East would bring in cheap Russian grain with catastrophic results for agriculture, particularly in Bohemia. In this attitude, they were supported by the extreme German nationalists who liked an opportunity to act as defenders of the peasants and who did not like a bill that was to confer advantages on the Slavic lands of Cisleithania. In addition, the agrarian speakers expressed their general distrust of industrialization. But in the debate as a whole, the opposing voices were drowned in a chorus of approval, and the "feudals" had to confine themselves to the futile gesture of leaving the chamber when the bill was being voted upon. Koerber intervened in the debates a couple of times to reiterate his view that he avoided all optimism regarding the profitability of the canals but was certain that the economy as a whole would reap generous interests from the waterways. In talking about the finances of the plan, he stressed that the burdens would increase very gradually as the needs arose, and he referred approvingly to Boehm-Bawerk's declaration before the Parliament that "we shall not allow a deficit to re-enter our budget," a sentence the House cheered.[53] In view of the subsequent developments, this statement is of particular importance, and we shall return to it. To anticipate here, it may reveal a dangerous chink in Koerber's armor. What he was trying to do was to engineer a spurt, a discontinuity in Austria's economic evolution, and he appeared content to meet this discontinuity by a gradual approach, that is to say, by a continuity in financing a discontinuous project. This crucial problem will be discussed mainly in Lecture Three.

Some speakers in the debate, also those otherwise very favorably disposed, could not help criticizing the speed with which the

---

[52] *Stenographisches Protokoll, Haus der Abgeordneten*, Session XVII, Meeting 52 (May 29, 1901), pp. 4425-4428.

[53] *Stenographisches Protokoll, Haus der Abgeordneten*, Session XVII, Meeting 52 (May 29, 1901), and Meeting 56 (June 3, 1901), pp. 4477, 4874.

bill was "whipped" through the house and even more so the lack of specifics both in the bill and in the report of the committee. The point was well taken. Even the official motivation (which accompanied every bill and explained its background and purposes) submitted to the Parliament by the government, had to admit that the "total costs of the canal constructions cannot be determined even in an approximate fashion today," and confined itself to the generality that "a too far-reaching burden upon State credit will be excluded according to human foresight."[54]

But not only total financial needs appeared uncertain. From a technological point of view, the preparations for the canal construction appeared quite incomplete. The technical methods to be used in overcoming differentials in altitudes were still under discussion. That meant that the precise course of the canals, dependent as it was upon agreement on technology, had to remain open and required further study. This was surprising because the technicians in the Ministry of Commerce, had been working on the canal project and particularly on the Danube-Oder Canal for years. These uncertainties were freely admitted by Baron Call, the Minister of Commerce, in his intervention in the debate when he remarked somewhat feebly that while it was true that the engineers were still arguing, progress was bound to result from such disagreements.[55]

But to return to the Czechs whose conversion and decision to stop obstruction was crucial for the passage of the bill. Kramář claims a great deal of credit for the Czech contribution to the bill. "I must assert," he said, "that it was we, and only we who made out of the government canal bill an act regarding river regulations." He still felt, in 1906, that the decision to stop obstruction was to be apologized for, and he mentions the "price" that the government paid the Czechs for doing so (the erection of a Gallery of Modern Art in Prague). But price or no price, the fact is that the Czech politicians were unable to resist for nationalistic purposes (language question, Bohemian State Law, etc.) some-

[54] *Stenographisches Protokoll, Haus der Abgeordneten*, Session XVII, Beilagen, Nr. 792, p. 13.

[55] *Stenographisches Protokoll, Haus der Abgeordneten*, Session XVII, Meeting 53 (May 5, 1901), p. 4579.

thing that was to confer real economic benefits upon the population. The pressures upon them were strong indeed. As Kramář says: "Besides, we negotiated with the Germans regarding the workability of the Bohemian diet, and that was in that summer [of 1901]—we can admit it now—a matter of extraordinary importance to us. For without an act of the Diet regarding the provinces' contribution to the regulation of the Elbe and Moldau Rivers . . . a matter which has inestimable value for our economic development, nothing short of a catastrophe was threatening." And the final—in fact, the crucial—admission was as follows: "I do not want to mention that our People hardly would have tolerated for a long time such an endless, groundless opposition. For, like every other People, it expects from the Parliament positive, primarily economic labors."[56] One must note that the last quotation echoed strongly Koerber's reply to the Czech abuse in the Parliament of his economic program, as offered in 1900.[57]

This was the best summary of what happened in 1901. Koerber, and with him the economic interests of the population, won over the politics of nationalism. The victory was by no means confined to the economic bills, or rather Koerber of the economic bills proved to be the master. On December 18, 1901, the Parliament accepted the provisional budget, and, finally, after an orderly conducted debate in which Koerber did not fail to mention that the budget for 1902 also contained 75 million crowns for the projects stipulated under the Canal Act, the house passed the 1902 budget on May 23, 1902. This was the first time a budget was constitutionally adopted after the crisis that followed the Badenis decrees and their withdrawal. It is true that in the interval in December 1901 Koerber felt that he should hint that return of obstruction might cause the government to have recourse to extraordinary measures, but rumors of an impending coup d'état or dissolution of the Parliament were effectively quashed by Koerber within three days, thus finishing what proved to be an insignificant episode.

There can be no doubt, however, that in that spring of 1902

---

[56] Karl Kramář, *Anmerkungen*, pp. 50, 59-60, 69.

[57] *Stenographisches Protokoll, Haus der Abgeordneten*, Session XVI, Meeting 39 (March 2, 1900), p. 2597.

Two: Economic Backwardness

Koerber had reached the acme of his success and influence. He had achieved what no one had believed could be achieved. Any wish of Koerber's would be gladly satisfied by a grateful and admiring Emperor. Those summer months that followed the vote of the budget were the most decisive, crucial months in Koerber's career as Prime Minister. This cannot be stressed too strongly, because for reasons I will discuss later, this is not understood by those writing on the history of that period. The fact is that after that May day of 1902 Koerber stood on a high plateau. But there are few plateaus in the Austrian Alps, and, whenever the hiker reaches one, he must either ascend or descend. And that was precisely what lay before Koerber. He knew by what means he had reached his height. He should have known that to aspire to still higher heights required another injection and probably a very generous injection into the body economic of the country of the healing and invigorating stuff that he had administered in the past.

Thus the whole problem of the Koerber program, of its success or failure, was concentrated in those fateful months in the decision to be taken. To understand the historical fate of the Koerber program is to understand the reasons that prevented action and determined inaction in the summer months of 1902. Lecture Three will offer some insight into this central problem.

The Stumbling Block

IN THIS LECTURE, the hero of the previous two lectures becomes a non-hero, while the role of the anti-hero is played, collectively speaking, by the Austrian Ministry of Finance and, personally speaking, by its head, Eugen von Boehm-Bawerk, the Minister of Finance. Before deciding, in the spring of 1901, to submit the Canal Bill to the Parliament, Koerber had to secure Boehm-Bawerk's consent to the allocation of the funds needed. Accordingly, as Sieghart quotes from his diary: "At Pentecost, Koerber sent me to Boehm-Bawerk who at that time happened to dwell in Abbazia [on the Adriatic Sea] in order to persuade him to make for *political* reasons a sacrifice to his convictions and to agree to the amount of 250 million crowns to be inserted in the Canal Bill. Boehm-Bawerk agreed, whereupon the Canal Bill was submitted."[1] As we shall see presently, there was a crying inconsistency between the grandeur of the bill (particularly as it was voted on by the Parliament in a greatly amplified form) and the amount of finance designed to cover it.

My suspicions about the obstructive and destructive position and policies of the Ministry of Finance with regard to the Koerber experiment were first aroused by a significant passage in the memoirs of Alexander Spitzmueller, who at that time was a high civil servant in the Ministry of Finance and claims to have been Boehm-Bawerk's confidant (*Vertrauensmann*) in the most important reforms.[2] Spitzmueller's passage reads as follows: "The in-

[1] Cf. Rudolf Sieghart, *Die letzten Jahrzehnte einer Grossmacht*, p. 58. Italics supplied. The quotation in the text does not include what Sieghart has to say about Koerber's own attitude to the Canal Bill. This will be dealt with later. Italics supplied.

[2] Alexander Spitzmueller, . . . *und hat auch Ursach, es zu lieben*, Vienna, 1955, p. 47. The author, born in 1862, was 90 years old on the day he wrote the preface to the book, but he appears to have been blessed with an excellent memory and had an assistant check his dictations against his diaries. Thus, even though the memoirs were composed nearly half a century after the events treated in these lectures, there is little doubt that they deserve very serious attention.

vestment projects of Herr von Koerber laid very strong claims upon the finances of the State and in their original formulation would have led to a serious (*bedenklich*) over-extension of state credit. *Sektionschef* Dr. Gruber [another top civil servant in the Ministry] even foresaw the danger of a recurring inflationary degeneration of the finances of state. Herr von Boehm, who wished to restrict as little as possible the *political conception* of the chief of the cabinet, but on the other hand shared fully the financial apprehensions, got thereby into a very difficult situation. Quite naturally, I, too, was pulled into the situation, being the [Ministry's] representative at the relevant negotiations. I succeeded in fact to curtail the canal project very strongly, so that particularly the Danube-Oder Canal never got beyond the stage of intensive preliminary labors and projects. Koerber seemed to regard me as the soul of the resistance to a too far-reaching investment policy, and I believe that at that time I lost my position in his eyes which till then had been a very favorable one."[3]

After reading this passage, I decided to spend several weeks in the Archives of the Ministry of Finance in Vienna (*Finanzarchiv*), located in Prince Eugene's Inner City palace, whose magnificent baroque staircase stands out in a town that has no scarcity at all of lovely baroque buildings. Received with customary Viennese courtesy and greatly aided by the small but knowledgeable staff of the Archive, I needed a few days to burrow my way to the relevant files, whereupon I could devote myself to deciphering the documents found. In those days, when the century was so very young, the Ministry, as a rule, used no typewriters and everything *was written in long hand in Gothic script, that was rendered more illegible* by the fact that both the Minister and his top aides knew each other's handwriting so well that their contributions to the files were composed in a hastily written and highly personalized scrawl. Only the letters leaving the Ministry were entrusted to a calligraphic scribe. Curiously enough, no true copies of those let-

---

[3] *Ibid.*, p. 49. Italics supplied. This sigh of a bureaucrat, keen on making his career, need not touch us too deeply. But it must be appreciated how much backing by his chief, Boehm-Bawerk, the young civil servant must have expected, if he was willing to risk the favors of a powerful Prime Minister by opposing the latter's policy.

ters were preserved, and the drafts with their various insertions and corrections served as the copy. If before signing the final copy of an outgoing letter, some change, be it ever so slight, occurred to the Minister, at least in principle, a special short memorandum incorporating the change had to be prepared and added to the drafts as a separate sheet. The system was not remarkable for its efficiency, but it does give the researching student a view of the documents in the making and an insight into the individual positions taken by the Minister and his aides.

The following presents either summaries of or, when advisable, quotations from the relevant documents. In some cases quotations *in extenso* have been deemed necessary. Let me begin at the beginning, that is to say at the interdepartmental conferences dealing with the drafting of the Canal Bill of 1901. Such conferences took place on March 27 and March 30, 1901, in the Ministry of Commerce, and were conducted by the Minister of Commerce, Baron von Call. If the Prime Minister was present, the files make no mention of it. In these conferences, Spitzmueller tried hard to frighten the participants by speaking of the dire financial consequences of the bill. He mentioned "confidentially," as he said, that a government loan would have to be issued to cover the cost of acquisition of new cannons, which, together with railroad investments, would provide all the strain on the budget that could be tolerable for the current decade. "I do not wish to point out to you what it would mean if at the same time also a loan for canal construction were to be floated." "Even now the banking circles are already fearful, lest the already proposed investments [in railroads] should force us to have recourse to the European capital market. In such a case our political conditions in the last few years would come to affect unfavorably the terms under which such a loan could be obtained." "For these reasons the Ministry of Finance is opposed to a loan and would prefer creation of a [slowly growing] special fund." With a good dramatic sense, Spitzmueller also spoke of "an enormous damage to our credit" and, at the second meeting, did not hesitate to envisage "a catastrophe for our finances."

His colleague at the Ministry of Finance, Baron Friedrich von Raymond, stated in less emotional language the reasons for the traditional negative attitude of the Ministry of Finance toward canal projects. The general points of his speech will appear further below in the memorandum on the subject that he later submitted to Boehm-Bawerk. For the rest, the representatives of the Ministry raised a multiplicity of objections. The period of construction of canals was not to be confined to fifteen years, as originally stipulated in the bill, but should extend to twenty years. Similarly, construction should not start in 1904, but be delayed to 1906. Much energy was expended on trying to excise from the bills such terms as "immediately" (with regard to the commencement of negotiations with the provinces about their contributions to the cost of canals) and the like. The idea of establishing a non-governmental autonomous commission with some power of administering the canals was strenuously objected to because the Ministry of Finance would have little or no influence upon such a body. The various objections by the Ministry led to the establishment of a subcommittee of the conference in which the differences were again argued out. In the end a compromise of sorts resulted. The Ministry was defeated on the year in which construction was to begin and also on its resistance to the loan that was incorporated in the bill. By contrast, the Ministry succeeded in lengthening the period of construction to twenty years and also in having the autonomous commission replaced by a supposedly merely consultative body (*Beirat*) to be set up by the Ministry of Commerce, to whose agenda canals naturally belonged.

What matters from the point of view of this study is that, from the outset, the Ministry of Finance adopted the policy of delays and procrastinations vis-à-vis the canals, that is to say a policy that in the Austrian bureaucratic jargon went under the very familiar name of *dilatorische Taktik*. It would seem, therefore, that the Ministry did not object so much to the provision of funds by a loan as to the lost possibility to defer the question of funds to a separate act to be passed in 1905, which, as Raymond mentioned in his memorandum (Folio 8), would have preserved at least theoretically the possibility of *not* beginning the construction of this or that canal.[4]

[4] For the preceding as well as for the following remarks on Raymond's memorandum, see *Finanzarchiv*, G.Z. 1845/10.1 *ex* 1901. Note that *all* citations from *Finanzarchiv* refer to what is known as *Praesidialakten*.

Three: Stumbling Block

Thus it appears that the files in the Archive do support the passage quoted from Spitzmueller's memoirs, but they do not do so completely. It certainly is correct that the Ministry of Finance tried to curtail the canal bill and that the compromise achieved took some account of its objections. But the passage is incorrect in stressing Spitzmueller's central role in the debates. He was indeed outspoken and injected most of the drama into the preliminary debates. But the crucial part was played not by Spitzmueller, but by Baron Raymond. Nor do the files, as far as I could see, bear any traces of Spitzmueller's subsequent actions in the matter. These, too, were mostly undertaken by Raymond.

Boehm-Bawerk did not participate in the drafting conferences. It seems, however, that after the passage of the two investment bills, Boehm-Bawerk (possibly at a cabinet meeting) expressed himself orally on the whole subject, warning against exceeding the cost estimates and arguing that, should an economic or political crisis break out, all the work on constructions be stopped. Thereafter the head of the Railroad Ministry, Wittek, felt impelled to write to Boehm-Bawerk to emphasize that any such stoppage of constructions would expose the government to suits for damages on the part of the contractors. With regard to remaining within the cost estimates, Wittek declared his intention to do so as far as feasible (*tunlichst*), but went out of his way to tell the Minister of Finance that the investment projects would open up new areas of production, create new industries, evoke technological progress—all this bringing forth additional financial needs that could not be foreseen.

Wittek's letter is nothing short of a lesson in dynamics of economic development taught by the experienced railroad man who appreciated the need for flexibility and bigness to a statically minded and rather pettily inflexible warden of the State Treasury.[5] This is an important letter, because it shows that Boehm-Bawerk even at that early date was quite willing to envisage a discontinua-

[5] *Finanzarchiv*, 2884/10.1 *ex* 1901. Wittek's letter bears the date of June 24, 1901. During the drafting conferences, Wittek had argued strongly that the original cost estimates, particularly for canals, are usually insufficient and must be exceeded. The point was exceedingly well taken, as it is supported by the history of nearly all canals built in North America, whether large projects like the Erie and Welland Canals or small canals or canalizations of rivers.

tion, that is to say failure, of the investment projects and was leaving a free hand for himself to use a future unspecified crisis for the purpose. That an *economic* crisis could be thought to require cessation of governmental investment activities is not surprising within the intellectual climate of the period. Something more will have to be said on this point later.

The previously cited file (1845/10.1 *ex* 1901) contains a longish memorandum that Raymond submitted to his Minister. The memorandum is of interest because it reveals the intensity of the antagonistic feelings on the subject of canals, which, as Raymond said, did not derive from fiscal reasons alone, but were also based on considerations regarding technology, communications, and economic policy in general. The main points may be summarized as follows: (1) canals may be justifiable in other countries, but in Austria both geography (elevations to overcome) and climate militate against canals. (2) As a result, canal construction in Austria requires much higher investment outlays, and along with the high cost of construction goes the high cost of operation, which prevents the claimed advantage of lower freight from materializing. At the same time, artificially low fees for canal users will fail to safeguard proper returns on capital investment, and the canals may come to operate at an outright loss. (3) The alleged enhanced opportunities for exports via canals will be offset by enhanced opportunities for cheaper imports into Austria of agricultural and industrial commodities in competition with domestic production. (4) The alleged cheaper availability for Vienna and Lower Austria of coal from northern provinces to be brought on the Danube-Oder Canal may in reality favor not Vienna, but Budapest and Hungary in general, because of the lower freight rates down the Danube. (5) The envisaged canal system will favor the port of Hamburg at the expense of Triest and is thus inconsistent with the construction of the second rail connection with Triest and expansion of the latter port. (6) Canals will put industries that are remote from the canals and still using rail transportation at a disadvantage and make them demand adjustment of freight rates on the railroads down to the freight rates on the canals; state-owned railroads will be unable to resist such demands, thus devaluing the capital invested in the railroads.

Three: Stumbling Block

The last point shows with particular clarity that Raymond would use any argument against canals; his mind was not warped by a false ambition of consistency, so he could envisage both canals operating at intolerably high cost and their successful competition against the railroads. It should also be noted that nowhere in the memorandum is there any reference to possible divergencies between micro-profitabilities and macro-advantages of the whole scheme. Nor is there any appreciation of the need for economic development. Again, one must call attention to the fact that neither Sieghart, in trying to induce Boehm-Bawerk to agree to the outlays (*vide supra*), nor Spitzmueller, in describing Boehm-Bawerk's attitude, spoke of anything else but the "political reasons" behind the Koerber plan (meaning cessation of obstruction in the Parliament). Nothing was said of the value of the plan for the economic progress of the country.

While the Ministry of Finance persisted in its hostile attitude, public opinion was deeply moved by the canal scheme. To some extent, Raymond's memorandum polemicized against an article that had appeared more than a month earlier in the *Neue Freie Presse*. The latter was the leading Viennese newspaper and, in fact, the only Austrian newspaper of European format and significance. The paper had close connections with the world of industry, commerce, and banks. The article greeted the canal project with unrestrained enthusiasm.[6] It asserted that the economic importance of the project vastly exceeded that of the Tauern Railroad. "There is no industry which does not place great hopes in the construction of canals." The scheme was said to have changed the evaluation of the economic conditions and prospects by merchants and industrialists with one fell blow, meaning that the pessimism engendered by the depression of 1900 was being quickly dissipated.

Somewhat later appeared the usual annual report of the Chamber of Commerce and Industry in Vienna for the year 1900.[7] Following the quick and unexpected adoption of the Canal Bill by

[6] *Neue Freie Presse*, March 10, 1901.

[7] Handels- und Gewerbekammer in Wien, *Bericht ueber die Industrie, den Handel und die Verkehrsverhaeltnisse in Nieder-Oesterreich waehrend des Jahres 1900*, Vienna, 1901, p. XXIV.

the Parliament, the authors of the report joyously transcend the limits of the previous calendar year in order to stress the economic importance of the scheme and to mention the labors in this direction by the relevant associations, including a great special conference with representatives from all provinces clamoring for canals, and the fact that the powerful Industrial Council (*Industrierat*) has added its voice in demanding the construction of canals. The report goes on to emphasize the value of the canals for numerous industries as well as the direct importance of constructions in providing employment for years to come.

These public reactions in favor of the canals are significant because they meant that the Ministry of Finance was isolated in its antagonism and had to proceed in intra-ministerial secrecy, always fearful lest its opposition would come to the ears of the public. This aspect of the matter will appear more clearly presently.

At the same time, Boehm-Bawerk wrote to the Minister of Commerce asking to be currently informed on the canal projects and concluded by saying: "Allow me to request that in assessing the amounts for the preliminary studies which according to article 12 of the Law are directly charged to the budget, the greatest possible thrift be used, inasmuch as an unjustifiably large charge to the annual budget from this source must be avoided under all conditions in view of the budgetary situation with which Your Excellency are perfectly familiar."[8]

Call's reply came four months later containing first the statement that he was not yet in a position to present a formal program and then assuring the Minister of Finance that he, too, "firmly adhered to the obvious principle in accordance with which the appropriate (*ressortmaessig*) influence of the Ministry of Finance in the matter of canal construction will be at all times safeguarded with regard to all measures of financial consequence and in general in every financially significant phase of the matter." Call followed this piece of ministerial courtesy by suggesting the creation of a—naturally merely *internal*—inter-ministerial committee composed of representatives of the ministries involved as the most suitable way to achieve agreements *more easily and more quickly*.

[8] *Finanzarchiv*, 2823/10.1 *ex* 1901.

Three: Stumbling Block

In conclusion Call wished "to assure Your Excellency that I, too, am deeply concerned with the application of greatest possible thrift both with regard to the organization [to set up] as well as to the preliminary studies, insofar as such thrift will be compatible with the administration of the tasks prescribed by the Law of June 11, 1901."[9]

The letter is rather defensive in tone. Hearts certainly became faint whenever Boehm-Bawerk referred to the "budgetary situation," and any deficit, be it never so negligible, produced a frightening effect upon the minds of the cabinet. It is, therefore, all the more interesting that the concluding paragraph contains a thinly disguised warning to Boehm-Bawerk not to interfere with the duty devolving upon the Minister of Commerce to execute faithfully a duly passed law. The suspicion that the Minister of Finance might be willing to break the law is likely to have fleeted through Baron Call's mind, a suspicion not entirely unfounded, as we shall see. The reference to thrift in organizing the legally prescribed council (*Beirat*) and in preliminary studies is actually too trifling for words, considering that both expenditures were to amount to 141,000 crowns (as reported by Call to the budget committees of the Parliament) and that in relation to a project whose cost was to amount first to 250 million crowns and eventually altogether to 750,000 crowns, plus or minus (*rund*).[10] Boehm-Bawerk's reaction to Call's suggestion regarding an internal Ministerial Committee is also worth recording. The Minister of Finance was not against establishment of such a committee, but only if the Ministry of Finance had been given full opportunity for careful study of the problems involved; therefore, the committee should deal with those problems *after* the Ministry had finished its study and the agreement between the Ministry of Commerce and the Ministry of Finance had been achieved. Since Call's idea in proposing the committee was to expedite matters and to make for an "easier and quicker" meeting of minds, Boehm-Bawerk's

[9] Letter of October 30, 1901, Ministry of Commerce, Zahl 2721; *Finanzarchiv*, 4739/10.1 *ex* 1901. Italics supplied.

[10] *Stenographisches Protokoll, Haus der Abgeordneten*, Session XVII, Beilagen, Nr. 792. It is true that the expenditures in question would have been direct charges to the budget, but certainly adjustable later.

reply amounted to an outright rejection of the proposal and clearly denoted his intention to obstruct and procrastinate.[11]

It should be in order to mention at this point a rather ambiguous weapon that the Ministry of Finance kept in reserve to be used in its campaign against the canal project. This was the rather darkly drafted article 11 of the Law of June 11, 1901. The article read as follows: "In order to provide cover for the annuity burden resulting from the floatation of the loan the Minister of Finance has, before the beginning of construction, if appropriate (*gegebenenfalls*), to submit proposals for constitutional treatment." Neither the legislative history of the article nor its precise meaning is clear to me. The term "constitutional treatment" is lucid enough, meaning adoption of a law to be duly passed by the Parliament. But the meaning of "*gegebenenfalls*" is ambiguous. It may mean "if appropriate," but also "should occasion arise" or "should the need arise." Nor does the article say who was to determine the appropriateness or the occasion or need. If this was to be the Minister of Finance, then the duty the act imposed upon him by this article was a highly contingent one. At any rate, neither the failure of the minister to submit a bill nor a failure of Parliament to pass it, it appears, would have any practical consequences for the orderly administration of the Canal Act. Nevertheless, as will be shown later, the Minister of Finance could, and actually did, regard the article in question as a possible instrument of delaying, if not undermining, the Canal Act.

Because, as described in Lecture Two, Koerber failed to utilize the favorable situation in 1902 for placing the canal project upon a new, greatly amplified legislative basis, the treatment of the project proceeded within the framework of the Act of June 11, 1901, whose financial inadequacy very soon appeared clear. In October 1901 the Ministry of Commerce issued a decree establishing within the ministry a special *Direction for the Construction of Canals* and appointing the legally foreseen Waterways Council (the previously mentioned *Beirat*). The latter was to be composed of 40 members, half of them to be appointed by the ministries involved and the other half by the Executive Committees of the provinces concerned, the appointees being partly deputies and partly representatives of various branches of the economy. A cir-

---

[11] For Boehm-Bawerk's reply, see *Finanzarchiv*, 2823/10.1 *ex* 1901.

cumstance that awoke the displeasure of the Ministry of Finance was that the *Beirat* was given the right to pass resolutions and thus was to be more than a merely consultative body. Also, the large size of the *Beirat* was unfavorably commented upon within the ministry, because the public—so much in favor of the canals—received a large representation.[12]

Before I deal with the activities of the *Beirat*, of whose annual plenary meetings stenographic records were preserved, I must first address myself to the memorandum (*Denkschrift*) of the Ministry of Commerce that was issued in June 1902 (with a brief supplement dated December 1902).[13]

The development of a construction program for the "first period," 1902–1912, required answers for the following three questions: 1) the size of monetary funds available; 2) the selection of projects to be started during this period; and 3) the mode of distributing the funds among the individual construction projects.

The Canal Act allocated a loan of 250 million crowns to the first period. Out of this nominal sum, 75 million crowns were to be devoted not to canals proper, but to river regulations. The memorandum assumes throughout a loss of five percent in the floatation of the loan (the difference between nominal values and effective yields). Accordingly, about 78,948,000 crowns had to be floated in order to secure the amount of 75 million crowns. Thereby the nominal amount available for the canal construction is reduced to 171 million crowns, this representing the seven-eights of the total to be supplied by the state. Adding to this amount the one-eighth to be supplied by the provinces, the memorandum arrives at the nominal amount of 195.5 million, which finally leaves an effective amount of 185.7 million crowns.

The second canal was to connect the Danube with the Moldau at Budweis in Bohemia, and the Moldau River to be canalized from Budweis to Prague.[14] Unfortunately the question whether the Danube-Moldau Canal should start from Vienna or from Linz

[12] For the decree of October 11, 1901, see *Reichsgesetzblatt* 163 *ex* 1901.

[13] *Denkschrift des Handelsministeriums ueber das Bauprogramm der durch das Gesetz vom 11. Juni 1901 sichergestellten Wasserstrassen in der ersten Bauperiode 1904 bis 1912.*

[14] Curiously, the wording of the Act "to Prague" (*bis Prag*) raised the problem whether this "to" did or did not mean "through Prague." After some soul searching, the ministry decided on the more generous interpretation.

(the capital of Upper Austria) had not yet matured to a decision status, and accordingly, only the canalization of the Moldau was to be included in the program. No explanation was offered in the memorandum on the failure to reach a decision. In addition, it was also decided to carry through a canalization of the Elbe River.

As far as the construction of actual artificial waterways (canals) is concerned, the memorandum mentions the technical difficulties of construction, that is the elevations to be overcome within short stretches.[15] For these reasons and because of the much greater general economic importance of the Danube-Oder Canal, the authors of the memorandum believed that the greatest possible degree of completion of this canal during the period 1901–1912 should be aimed at, along with a connection between that canal and the Vistula at the city of Cracow in Galicia.

According to the memorandum, the available effective amount of 185.7 million crowns was to be distributed as follows (figures in million crowns):

Canalization of Moldau	14.4
Canalization of Elbe	37.0
Cracow-Donau-Oder Canal	30.0
Donau-Oder Canal	104.3
Total	185.7[16]

The memorandum leaves its readers under no illusion as to the magnitudes of these allocations. During the preparation of the act the total expenditure over twenty years was to amount *at least* to 750 millions, and in many quarters 800 million crowns was judged to be a more likely amount. Thus, 45 percent (9 years) of the total construction period of twenty years had at their disposal less than 25 percent of the total amount to be expended on the canals. It must also be noted that the cost of the Danube-Oder Canal was computed as a residual, after having assessed the

[15] The Danube-Oder Canal had to overcome a difference in altitude of 205 meters over a stretch of 275 kilometers. The corresponding figures for the connection between the Danube-Oder Canal and the Elbe River were 400 and 180; while the Danube-Moldau Canal, if starting from Vienna, had to rise 500 meters over 200 kilometers, and if, starting from Linz, even 600 meters over only 120 kilometers. These figures are supposedly more precise than those previously given in 1901 (see Lecture Two n. 50).

[16] *Denkschrift*, p. 48.

Map of Rivers and Places,
mentioned in the text.
Especially Prepared for This Study by
Doctor Hans Slanar, Cartographer
in Vienna, Austria

97

amounts for the three other projects. The reader of the memorandum cannot help feeling that it studiously avoided significant details, remaining quite silent on the prospective course of the Danube-Oder Canal, so that one had to rely on the daily press for some information on the subject. The problem raised by the memorandum and especially the size of funds available for the individual constructions naturally were discussed at the plenary sessions of the *Beirat*, to which we will devote some attention now, as they bear directly on the problem Koerber faced, or refused to face, in 1902.

Little can be said about the first two plenary meetings of the *Beirat* late in 1901 and in the spring of 1902. The agrarians demanded stronger representation on the *Beirat*, in order to push their view that river regulations were much more important than canals; other members stressed that agrarian interests were distrustful of the Canal Act as a whole. In opposition to the agrarians it was also argued that the dichotomy of regulations versus canal construction was a false one, as the construction of the Danube-Oder Canal would involve the regulation of the long stretch of the March River between Lower Austria and Moravia and into Moravia. These were rather inconclusive debates back and forth, and the members did not seem to have any feeling that the whole enterprise was in a rather critical state. The atmosphere of extreme optimism in which the Canal Act had been passed apparently prevailed undiminished and prevented the members from seeing any problems or anticipating dangers.

By contrast, the third plenary meeting of the *Beirat* was free of any complacency. It was held on the last of January 1903, that is, after the publication of the *Denkschrift* of the Ministry of Commerce. Suddenly, there was a sense of urgency. The law failed to specify any sequence in initiating the projects envisaged. Hence, the question of priorities arose and threatened to divide the membership. The Danube-Oder Canal and the Danube-Elbe Canal suddenly were in a state of competition. The Viennese, the Moravians, and the Poles (Galicia!) plugged for giving priority to the Danube-Oder project, while the Bohemians (both the Germans and the Czechs) pushed for the competing project. In rather uncertain debates, it was argued whether the Silesian coal (Danube-

Oder) was more or less important economically than the Bohemian coal (Danube-Elbe).

Not unnaturally, the mayor of Vienna, Lueger, advocated giving priority to the Danube-Oder Canal with its projected starting point in Vienna. To support this position, he could refer to the *Denkschrift* of the Ministry of Commerce which, too, had favored concentration of efforts first on that canal. A skillful politician, Lueger did not forget to mention that all the nationalities, the Germans (in Lower Austria and Vienna), the Czechs (in Moravia), and the Poles (in Galicia), were interested in the Danube-Oder Canal. Lueger also rather effectively made use of what today is called the indivisibility argument, that is, that the economic value of an unfinished canal was close to zero; or, as Lueger put it in his colorful language: a short stretch from Vienna and a short stretch up from Ostrau (now Ostrava) would leave an economic Sahara in the middle; trying to bridge the gap by horse-driven traffic would raise the freight cost way above the present freight rates on the railroad. From time to time the discussions degenerated into the inane question as to whether the Silesian or the Bohemian owners of coal mines (they spoke of "coal barons") deserved more or less sympathy.

But slowly the debate reached the crucial point, which was the question of funds available. Lueger was asked whether he believed that the whole Danube-Oder Canal could be built at the cost of 104 million crowns, since the prospective contractors were demanding 180 million crowns, which was an assertion not further evidenced, but not implausible. The figure was stated independently by two speakers, the second one mentioning "at least 180 millions." The inadequacy of the available funds was further emphasized by reference to comparable German experience where much larger amounts were invested.

Several speakers referred to "bitterness" about the situation in their respective regions, and claimed that increasingly doubts about the seriousness of the whole canal project were beginning to spread through the population. The disagreements in the *Beirat* were certainly acrimonious. When Lueger's motion to concentrate on the Danube-Oder Canal was passed by the *Beirat*, the Bohemian delegates walked out in protest. Thus the canal project,

99

which had proved such a unifying force only one year earlier, was becoming a source of disunity, even though something of the old unifying spirit still remained in the midst of disagreements because both the Czechs and the Germans from Bohemia jointly pleaded for the Danube-Elbe connection.

Somewhat slowly the range of the *Beirat's* criticism widened to encompass the Ministry of Commerce and then the Canal Act itself. Lueger reproached the Minister, present at the meeting ex officio, with unduly extending the period of preliminary studies, and he urged beginning construction. More important was the growing comprehension that the legal terms must be changed. Max Menger, who had been the *rapporteur* on the bill in the Lower Chamber and considered himself in some sense the parliamentary father of the bill, sensed perhaps more clearly than others that the life of the child was in jeopardy. He, too, pleaded for concentrating on a big single project. To build several short canal stretches would make Austria a laughing stock in the world and would squander the now available money. Menger spoke of the high goals set by the legislative bodies in adopting the Canal Act. He reminded the *Beirat* that the act came about because several important interests in the relevant provinces had joined to make this law possible; and he pleaded for the spirit of cooperation to continue. The facts were clear: "That the sum [available at present] is insufficient is a matter of course." "It would be advisable therefore, for the gentlemen who are asking for larger amounts than those made available in the *first government program* to demand that the government apply to the Parliament with a request for further credits. That would be the correct way." "Now the task was to decide on one canal and then we shall and must find the means to start other canals." The parliamentary chances looked good to Menger: "Let us be frank, gentlemen, among ourselves. If the Germans, the Poles, and the Czechs are in agreement regarding a bill aiming, for instance, at an increase of construction funds, then it would be a strange matter indeed, if such a bill were not accepted by the Lower Chamber."

Menger's was a rather cogent argument, drawing the logical conclusion from the situation. Still there is something odd about his longish speech. First of all, it is not clear why he urged *others* to take some steps, while he himself refrained from making a motion that would place the *Beirat* on record as requesting the government to ask for additional funds. Second, it is surprising that Koerber's name was not mentioned at all during the debates. In the very midst of the Koerber era, the members of the *Beirat* should have naturally expected Koerber to act. Equally surprising is the failure on the part of everybody to raise the crucial question, that is, to wonder about Koerber's failure to approach the Reichsrat of his own volition. Although Koerber was not mentioned, another member of the cabinet was. The member from Galicia offered sharp strictures of the structure of the Canal Act with its two unequal periods of construction and altogether insufficient funds to cover the first period. He then added as an afterthought: "It is true, of course, that the Minister of Finance cited his reasons for which the market cannot be burdened with higher amounts." Thus, after critique of the Parliament the blame was squarely laid on Boehm-Bawerk. But, unlike so many other people, this particular member refused to regard Boehm-Bawerk as having said the last word on the subject. For he went on asking sharp rhetorical questions: "Shall we remain as we are? Shall a resolution [meaning the act] that is ludicrous for a great Empire be allowed to stay unchanged? This must be repaired." He went on to plead for a new spirit in the *highest* administration, thus presumably referring to Koerber, although still not mentioning him.[17]

And then? A year went by, and in February 1904 the *Beirat* met again for its fourth plenary session. Astonishingly little had changed in the interval. The members, Menger among them, continued to press for acceleration by the Ministry of Commerce. The member from Galicia again pleaded for higher funds, but did it in a much more restrained language. The Minister of Commerce, Call, replied rather feebly that he, too, was in favor of quickest completion of the canals [note the plural], curiously adding as the first reason the budgetary saving of the interim interest charges (the so-called *Interkalarzinsen*) and only in second place the desirability of earning as soon as possible the economic fruits of the whole enterprise. In reply to the request for additional funds, the Minister stated meekly and uncertainly that "the finances of the

[17] For the meetings of the *Beirat*, see *Stenographisches Protokoll, Wasserstrassen Beirat, Finanzarchiv*, XX. 1283 (18.941). Italics supplied.

state must be paid proper consideration, and that the present moment was *perhaps* [sic] not the most suitable to allow placing at an early point an increase in the construction capital in definite prospect." For the rest, the Minister added that so far the available funds had not been touched at all; that the actual work of digging had not begun; meaning that in these circumstances it was entirely too early to worry about insufficiency of funds. Finally, Baron Call said in a rather unabashed fashion that the highly important technical problem of how the canals should overcome the differentials in elevation (by locks or inclined planes) was as yet unsolved.[18]

No one at the meeting was willing to upbraid the Minister for the continued disagreements among his engineering staff. It will be remembered that in 1901 he lightly suggested that progress would result from such disagreements, but nearly three years later it was becoming clear that what the disagreements yielded was not progress but inability to arrive at decisions that had to precede action. And above all, there was in Call's speech the trembling reference to the budgetary necessities behind which stood the fears of the Minister of Finance. Nothing said at the meeting suggested the least comprehension that the whole Koerber experiment of which the canal project was such a *magna pars* was in gravest jeopardy and that, talking of the most suitable moment, it was quite possible that the moment had been irretrievably lost.

Nor was such comprehension visible in the sector of public opinion represented by the daily press. As one looks through the files of the *Neue Freie Presse* from Christmas 1902 through 1903, one cannot help being astonished at the great optimism about the future of the canal project. The interest remains persistent. In July 1903 almost every issue of the daily paper had something positive to say on the Danube-Oder Canal. On one of these days a rather detailed description of the course to be taken by the canal was published, including a reference to the crossing by the canal of a tributary of the March River, and then "over a mighty bridge" of the March River itself. The same article urged the highest speed in deciding whether the canal port in Vienna was to be located on the right or the left bank of the Danube. Because of flood dangers in-

[18] *Ibid.* Italics supplied.

volved, the problem apparently caused excitement in Vienna, but the paper insisted that disagreements of this sort should be settled in the general interest of the "Great Project."[19]

Was this positive attitude the result of Koerber's ability, with Sieghart's help, to keep the press in line? Or was the enthusiastic reception of the canal project continuing, as it were, by inertia? At any rate, there was a clear contrast between the mood of the press and the very subdued mood of the fourth session of the *Beirat* from which the aggressive exuberance of the preceding session had all but vanished. It should be noted, however, that neither the members of the *Beirat* nor the Ministry of Commerce were willing to admit that the canal project was seriously ailing, let alone moribund. There was no anticipation of the fact that after the 1904 session of the *Beirat* no less than four years would elapse before the fifth session would convene in 1908. The assumption—and apparently more than mere pretense—was that, despite the shortage of funds and the unresolved technological problems, the patient was doing well. This view was shared by both friends and foes. The latter, far from believing in any possibility of natural death, were busy mustering their forces and developing stratagems designed to impart a fatal blow to the whole project. Accordingly, we must return now to the Ministry of Finance.

The following story has been pieced together in its entirety from the files of the Ministry of Finance.[20] The story is not a pretty one. It deals with tenacious obstruction or sabotage of a law whose proper execution was a sworn duty of the Minister of Finance. It includes an admission of the willingness to break the law and, finally, an attempt, shrouded in great secrecy, to amend the

---

[19] *Neue Freie Presse*, December 25, 1902, July 14, 15, 17, 21, 22, and 23, 1903. It was also in July 1903 that Koerber, acting as Minister of Interior, wrote to Boehm-Bawerk to tell him that the "Vienna question" had not been clarified either technologically or with regard to the cost involved and that the Ministry of Interior was waiting for concrete proposals in both directions, and would then communicate with the Ministry of Finance. There was no sense of urgency or impatience in the letter, and, to judge by its tone, it was composed by a very relaxed and resigned Koerber. *Finanzarchiv*, 673/10.8, July 3, 1903.

[20] In one case only, some additional checking in the Administrative Archive *(Verwaltungsarchiv)* in Vienna, where the files of the Ministry of Commerce are kept, was done. For the appropriate reference *vide infra*, footnote 30.

Canal Act by replacing it by another, emasculated bill to be submitted to the Parliament; that attempt constituting an act of both personal and professional disloyalty toward the head of the cabinet, of which Boehm-Bawerk was a member. Reluctant as I am to overstrain my readers' patience, the extraordinary character of those actions makes it imperative to quote the relevant files *in extenso*.

It was not surprising that the demands raised at the third plenary session of the *Beirat* produced an almost immediate reaction from the Ministry of Finance. In a letter to the Minister of Commerce, Boehm-Bawerk stated firmly that he was unable to agree to any further appropriations. Raising the question would result in the claims of the interested parties becoming boundless (*ins Ungemessene steigern*); funds would be squandered; and agitation for the Danube-Moldau Canal would receive a great impetus. Refusing to be "forced in an irrational fashion," Boehm-Bawerk added that "according to experience such large sums as already are available now could not, assuming rational conduct of construction, be fully utilized within a space of time that would be even shorter than the first period of construction."[21] Note Boehm-Bawerk's resistance to, and the fear of, alternative construction of the Danube-Moldau Canal which was pushed in rare harmony by both Czechs and Germans in Bohemia,[22] and as such constituted the very focus of Koerber's policy reconciling the two warring parties in Bohemia. But nowhere in the files of the Ministry of Finance is there the slightest indication of awareness of, or sensitivity for, the political aspect of the matter. This, just as economic development, was entirely outside the ministry's purview.

In June of 1903, the Minister of Commerce wrote to Boehm-Bawerk to suggest that the whole task of the first period might be finished within three to five (rather than nine) years. At once an indignant and inflexible Minister of Finance met with the Minister

[21] *Finanzarchiv*, 673/10.8. Letter of February 28, 1903.

[22] Cf. the articles by Victor Russ published after the meeting of the *Beirat*. *Neue Freie Presse*, February 18 and 21, 1903. At the same time, Czechs and Germans from Bruenn (now Brno), the capital of Moravia, also called on Koerber to urge the Danube-Oder Canal and its lateral extension to Bruenn. *Neue Freie Presse*, February 17, 1903.

of Commerce to object to such a "forced" speed of construction and to warn the Minister of Commerce against spending one *heller* (one crown was equal to 100 hellers), that is to say, not a penny, more than had been appropriated.[23]

In the late summer of 1903, the Ministry of Finance started working on a "financial program" to be presented to the Parliament under the terms of the previously discussed ambiguous article 11 that was being held back as the "secret weapon" of the ministry with the aim of delaying and perhaps diminishing the availability of the 250 million crowns as appropriated by the Canal Act for the first period of construction.[24]

A curious interlude occurred in the spring of 1904. It was hardly very important in itself, but cast sharp light on the atmosphere prevailing at the Ministry of Finance. A private consortium approached the ministry with a detailed proposal to build the Danube-Oder Canal and the connection to the Vistula River as a private undertaking without cost to the state, although requiring government guarantee for its bonds. The consortium would undertake to make the Danube-Oder Canal ready for traffic by the end of 1908 and to open up the connection to the Vistula by the end of 1910. The appropriated government funds thus set free could be used for construction of the other canals projected by the Canal Act. One would have expected the ministry to welcome a project that would have removed the Danube-Oder Canal from the state budget. This would require legislative action amending the Canal Act, and the consortium included in an extensive memorandum the draft of a bill to be used for the purpose. But the conclusion of the expert at the ministry who had been charged with a scrutiny of the proposals was altogether unexpected: "Without denying that an earlier completion of this water transportation project would be advantageous for the national economy, one may discern a danger rather than a gain in the possibility of using the relevant portion of the government loan for other purposes. . . . For [as a result of the legislative amendment] the endeavors aiming at an early construction of the Danube-Moldau Canal would receive new support," and the state would find itself in the danger of being pushed in that

[23] *Finanzarchiv*, 2961/10.8, June 26, 1903.
[24] *Finanzarchiv*, 3564/10.8, August 5, 1903.

direction. In this way, there might be no *real savings* for the budget.[25]

The proposals of the consortium remained without any practical consequence. They are interesting, however, inasmuch as they reveal on the one hand the almost irrational hostility of the ministry to the canal project and, on the other hand, its fear of the popular approval of, and enthusiasm for, the canals. For such fear lurked behind those references to desires and endeavors to be unleashed by legislative action. Despite all inflexibility and stress on dangers to budgetary stability, therein lay the weakness of Boehm-Bawerk's position, and obversely therein also lay Koerber's great potential strength, of which he had failed to make the proper use.

It was, however, the following summer of 1904 when things came to a head and the Minister of Finance got ready for a much more far-reaching action against the canal project. It all started with a news item in the *Neue Freie Presse*, shorter versions of which appeared in other daily papers and which had a bombshell effect within the Ministry of Finance. The item is reproduced here in translation with a few irrelevant, mostly toponymical omissions:

> The Prime Minister (*Ministerpraesident*) on the construction of waterways. Lately, many rumors were abroad according to which construction of waterways was to be delayed. Impelled by these rumors a delegation of Reichsrat deputies betook themselves to the Prime Minister and to the Minister of Commerce, in order to be informed whether construction of waterways will be begun still in the course of the current year. The Prime Minister and the Minister of Commerce stated to the deputies that no delay will take place in the construction of waterways. [The delegation consisted of members of Parliament who had been intensely concerned with subject of canals and very vocal at the sessions of the *Beirat*; among them were both Lueger and Menger.] The gentlemen went first to the Minister of Commerce, Baron Call, and thereupon to the Prime Minister, von Koerber. The Prime Minister completely cor-

[25] *Finanzarchiv*, 1011/10.1 *ex* 1904. Italics supplied.

roborated the information which the Minister of Commerce had given the delegation, and declared categorically (*mit aller Entschiedenheit*) that the construction of the canal from Vienna to Cracow will be started still this year in Lower Austria, as well as in Moravia and Galicia, and that the funds, requisite therefor, will be made liquid.

This paragraph was followed in the news item by the official statement, apparently issued by the office of the Prime Minister, the relevant parts of which read as follows:

The information offered by the Minister of Commerce reassured the gentlemen completely. In those provinces whose contribution to the cost of the project has been, in accordance with the Canal Act, assured by provincial legislation, that is to say in Lower Austria, Moravia, and Galicia, the work on detail project proceeds *pari passu*. As far as Lower Austria is concerned, the detail project for the partial stretch . . . [from Vienna onward] is essentially finished. And the negotiations with the ministers involved regarding agreement on the political *Begehung* [that is, an inspection of the terrain by representatives of the administration] have been initiated. With regard to the port in Vienna the recent resolutions of the Commission for the Regulation of the Danube have created the basis for locating the port in the old bed of the Danube [that is to say, on the left bank]. The technical department of the Direction for Construction of Waterways will work in contact with the technical organs of the Commission for the Regulation of the Danube. At any rate, there will be certain difficulties in solving the problem of simultaneous use of the old bed of the Danube for the port installation and for deflection when needed of the flood waters of the Danube. In Moravia large dams are to be built in order to assure the supply of water for the Danube-Oder Canal. The location of the dams will not be affected by the problem of the lifting works [in the Canal]. The dams and the reservoirs can and should be begun at once. The elaboration of the relevant detail projects is near completion. The completion of detail projects for the canal stretch . . . in Galicia is in full swing, and every effort is being made to finish them by August. These labors have been considerably handicapped by the small size of land properties and other local conditions in those areas. But everything is being done to accelerate the execution of those labors. The deputies raised the question of availability of means to cover the cost. The Minister replied that the Ministry of Commerce has at its disposal the sums required for the envisaged progress of construction. For the time being those sums will draw upon budgetary cash reserves to be refunded later from the proceeds of the loan. Finally, the Minister assured [the deputies] that in the three provinces mentioned all the dispositions have been made in order to begin construction still in the year 1904 as has been prescribed by the Canal Act.[26]

On the face of it, it was not obvious at all that the preceding official statement should give rise to any excitement. Under Article Six of the Canal Act it was explicitly and unambiguously stipulated that the construction of canals was to begin in 1904. The Prime Minister and the Minister of Commerce stated jointly that the stipulation of the law would be faithfully observed and, in order to reassure the parliamentarians, added that most, though not all of the preliminary problems had been either solved or were near solution; or, in other words, a situation existed that the government had been in duty bound to bring about. In fact, a statement to the effect that the work on the canals would *not* commence in 1904 would have allowed the Parliament to place the government under impeachment (*Ministeranklage*).

This, however, was not at all the position taken in the Ministry of Finance. With rather unbureaucratic haste, three days after the appearance of ministerial statements in the newspapers, Boehm-Bawerk had in his hands a seventeen-page memorandum prepared by the faithful Raymond. The author began by reference to the previous demand of the Ministry of Finance that no step going beyond the preliminary studies properly speaking should be undertaken in the canal matter without *previous* approval of the Ministry of Finance. This position was justified first as a question of "influence in itself" (*Ingerenz an sich*), then in view of the

[26] Cf. *Neue Freie Presse, Wiener Zeitung*, and *Die Reichswehr*, all three papers of June 17, 1904.

108

"enormous burden to be placed upon the finances of the State" by the execution of the Canal Act, and finally by the fact that at the time of the adoption of the act there existed neither technological projects nor cost estimates, and the situation required preliminary studies. Those studies, Raymond added, if carried out with the patience and thoroughness that the matter demanded, might well have led to the conclusion that it would have been better to desist from this or that canal construction. Thereupon Raymond spoke of the pressures generated by circles interested in the canal construction and charged the Technical Department of the Canal Direction with having for a long time encouraged those pressures by claiming that from a technical point of view everything was ready for starting the construction and that the delays experienced so far were only due to the restraining attitude of administrative organs [an obvious reference to the Ministry of Finance]. The unfortunate stipulation of Article Six of the Canal Act had created an inescapable situation (*Zwangslage*), which was all the more intolerable because, as was well known, the budgetary position of the state had become a great deal more difficult since the passing of the Canal Act. Accordingly, there was good reason to question the initiation of a program on whose economic value, to say the least, opinions diverged widely and whose financial consequences could not be foreseen at all.

So far the memorandum dealt with general cogitations that clearly revealed complete lack of respect for a constitutionally passed act. But Raymond went on to deal with the practical problem of policy to be pursued by the ministry. The main problem was to continue the policy of procrastination (*dilatorische Taktik*) which, as Raymond said, had been adopted "upon high order (*hohe Weisung*) of Your Excellency." This clear evidence that the policy in question had been originated by Boehm-Bawerk is worth noting. It also appears from the memorandum that in carrying out this procrastination the ministry had failed for at least two months to reply to a demand by the Ministry of Commerce to participate in the previously explained *politische Begehung* for the Danube-Oder Canal.

Raymond was not sure whether the policy of procrastination should be continued, although "formally" [that is to say, by re-

109

course to several pretexts] it could go on "for some time." On the other hand, it was to be feared first as a result of the official actions that must precede construction (*Begehungen* and land redemptions), second, because of the advent of the second half of 1904 and third because of the declarations of the Prime Minister and the Minister of Commerce, that a vehement agitation for the commencement of construction would be initiated and lead to a "first rate parliamentary question," whose settlement might result in further [financial] sacrifices of the state.

For these reasons, Raymond insisted that the only way to make the heavy burden upon the state treasury tolerable and at the same time drag out, and possibly even prevent, the beginning of construction was offered by Article 11 of the Canal Act. According to Raymond, it was possible to tie commencement of construction work to the parliamentary provision of funds under the terms of Article 11. And since Raymond was willing to interpret the inspection of terrain (*Begehung*) as the first step of construction work, even this inspection could be prevented until with the help of Article 11, as Raymond put it, "clear conditions would be established."[27]

These are the essential points of the memorandum that, to me at least, revealed for the first time the full extent and the full depth of the Ministry of Finance's hostility to Koerber's great plan. For the rest, it may be noted that the memorandum ailed from a curious inconsistency. On the one hand its author feared the public reaction to a continuation of the procrastination policy, which he surmised might even lead to an explosive situation in the Parliament as a result of which even larger funds would be appropriated in favor of the canal project. On the other hand, he counseled quite lightheartedly the reliance on Article 11, which would place the Minister of Finance before the Parliament in an attempt to make the legislature reduce or even rescind the already voted appropriation of 250 million crowns. A more provocative conduct would be hard to imagine.

At any rate, Boehm-Bawerk was certainly aroused by the dec-

[27] *Finanzarchiv*, 2418/10.8, June 20, 1904.

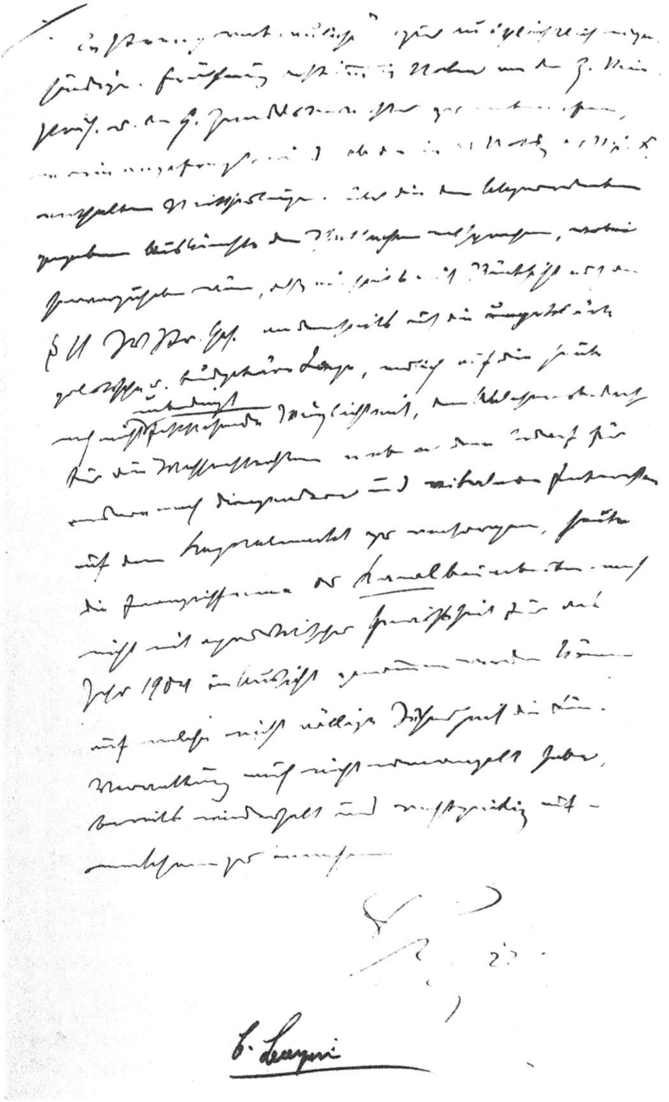

Boehm-Bawerk's Instructions, A Facsimile

larations of his chief, the Prime Minister, and his colleague, the Minister of Commerce. Two days after receiving Raymond's memorandum, he drafted stern instructions to his aide to draft a "strictly confidential letter for exclusively personal (*eigenhaendig*, by own hand) opening" to be sent to Koerber and Call.[28] In fact, there were to be two letters, the first paragraph of which differed inasmuch as in the letter to Koerber it referred to what the newspaper had attributed to the Prime Minister and in the letter to Call it referred to the corresponding attribution to the Minister of Commerce. Since those paragraphs restate the portions of the news item that has already been quoted, it is sufficient now to translate the main body of the letters whose text was identical. The letters were drafted by Raymond, but Boehm-Bawerk struck out some portions of the draft, inserting his own language, which then was duly incorporated in the final text, which was as follows:[29]

> I should be greatly obliged to Your Excellency for receiving information whether the data contained in the aforementioned news item do or do not correspond to facts.
>
> I for my part cannot hide the fact that it does not appear to me

[28] The sheet of Boehm-Bawerk's instructions is attached to the text in facsimile. Undisguised by Boehm-Bawerk's penmanship the sheet reads as follows: "Zu streng vertraulich. Zu ausschliesslich eigenhaendiger Eroeffnung bestimmte Noten an den Herrn Ministerpraesidenten und an Herrn Handelsminister zu unternehmen, worin angefragt wird, ob die in der Notiz der Neuen Freien Presse enthaltenen Mitteilungen ueber die den Abgeordneten gegebenen Auskuenfte den Tatsachen entsprechen, wobei hervorzuheben waere, dass einerseits mit Ruecksicht auf den Paragraph 11 des Wasserstrassengesetzes, andrerseits auf die ungeklaerte politische und budgetaere Lage, endlich auf die heute nicht unbedingt feststehende Moeglichkeit den Anlehensbedarf fuer die Wasserstrassen neben dem Bedarf fuer andere noch dringendere und vitalere Interessen auf dem Kapitalmarkt zu versorgen, heute die Inangriffnahme der Kanalarbeiten noch nicht mit apodiktischer Gewissheit fuer das Jahr 1904 in Aussicht genommen werden koenne, auf welche nicht voellige Sicherheit die Finanzverwaltung auch nicht ermangelt habe, bereits wiederholt und rechtzeitig aufmerksam zu machen."

[29] It should be in order to mention here that Boehm-Bawerk's books were written in a particularly beautiful and graceful German. It is fairly clear that he would leave this high gift outside the premises of the ministry. Boehm-Bawerk's official language is remarkable only for its heavy syntax and the flat choice of words. Accordingly, in translating the letter in the text an intolerably long sentence had to be split and readjusted in order to be made more readily intelligible.

established with apodictic certainty that it will be possible and permissible to proceed with the commencement of the work on the canals still in the course of the year 1904. [This is so for several reasons.] First, because of the stipulation of Article Eleven of the Waterways Act of June 11, 1901. Second, because of the unclear political and budgetary situation. Third, because today it is not yet unconditionally clear that it would be possible to obtain from the capital market the loan for the canals in addition to obtaining funds for other more urgent and more vital interests. And, finally, because of the complete uncertainty that has lasted until the present moment regarding the system upon which the canals are to be based (lifting mechanisms versus locks) and because of the complete lack of clarity regarding the prospective conditions of operation, costs and yields.

As Your Excellency will recall I have not failed, as the matter began to develop critically in the directions indicated, to raise my doubts and reservations as they related to my Ministry (*ressortmaessig*) first within the lap of the government and to urge agreement with the Ministry of Finance prior to taking steps that would prejudice the position outside the government.[30]

As we shall see later, Boehm-Bawerk did not wish to abandon altogether the possible use of Article 11, but the lightness and quickness of his touch in referring to that article in the letter may indicate his awareness of the inconsistency in Raymond's plea for reliance on it. Also the haughty, if not the authoritarian, fashion should be noted in which Boehm-Bawerk refers to matters such as the unclarified political and budgetary situation and the conditions of the capital market. He fails entirely to elaborate his assertions, and in particular his reference to "more urgent and more vital needs" to be satisfied by recourse to the capital market remains

[30] *Finanzarchiv*, 2418/10.8. Letters of June 29, 1904. Because of Boehm-Bawerk's corrections and the absence of a copy of the final text in *Finanzarchiv*, I had to check on the text in *Verwaltungsarchiv* where the letter bears the number P.Z. 434. G.P., and was no longer "strictly confidential" *(streng vertraulich)* but had become merely "confidential." Apparently, Boehm-Bawerk's correspondents felt somewhat less eager to protect the secrecy of Boehm-Bawerk's position.

quite unexplained, with the implication that Boehm-Bawerk's judgment as to what were the more urgent and more vital, though entirely unspecified, interests should take precedence over the Minister's duty to obey the law.

For the rest, Boehm-Bawerk's epistle elicited a mildly apologetic, but dignified reply from the Minister of Commerce, the main points of which are contained in the following translation:

Call began by acknowledging that he indeed had made the statements attributed to him by the *Neue Freie Presse* and proceeded to say that he felt entitled [he did not say "obliged"] to make those statements because the preliminary studies in his Ministry had reached such a stage that—barring unexpected impediments—it would be possible to comply with Article Six of the Canal Act in its prescription of the latest *terminus* for the beginning of construction.

> From the point of view of my Ministry I could not have very well said anything else without provoking public recriminations that would have claimed—and not without justice—that even the Ministry of Commerce did not take the canal project quite seriously.

> The stipulation of Article Eleven of the Canal Act [Call summarizes the article and underlines *gegebenfalls* appeared to me to have been rendered obsolete by the course of events. For Your Excellency has not so far submitted such proposals which under the terms of the law would have to be made before the beginning of construction (in 1904 at the latest).

> By contrast, Your Excellency had been good enough not only to approve for 1904 the estimate of 25 million crowns for construction purposes, but also had urged me repeatedly (for the last time in June 1904) to submit to you the estimates for 1905.

> I believed to be right in drawing from all those symptoms the conviction that Your Excellency did not consider the case of Article Eleven as given [*gegeben*, note the reference to *gegebenfalls*], so that no hindrances to the beginning of construction would arise from the legal stipulation of Article Eleven. It is, therefore, with regret that I must note that Your

Three: Stumbling Block

Excellency regards the observance of the legally prescribed beginning of construction as rendered questionable by the unclarified political and budgetary situation as well as by the uncertain aspects of the floatation of the Canal loan.

As far as concerns the uncertainty as emphasized by Your Excellency with regard to the technical system upon which the canals are to be based (lifting mechanisms versus locks) I believe to be able to dissipate those doubts. Of the canals prospected for the first period of construction it is only a partial stretch of the Danube-Oder Canal where lifting mechanisms for the ships could be considered at all. Yet even there such mechanisms would be by no means of vital importance because it had been established with full certainty that also the stretch in question could be built with locks. Hence, even if the public bids should fail to yield a positive result, this could affect the choice between the two systems but never the construction of the canal itself.

As far as the questions of prospective conditions of operation, costs, and yields are concerned, these things touching on the profitability of canals are in my opinion no longer of decisive significance after construction of canals has become a matter decided by the law. I believe, therefore, that the problem of lifting mechanisms, even though as yet unsolved, cannot possibly provide a motivation for postponing the beginning of construction inasmuch as the first canal stretch to be built— Vienna-Cracow—will be, under all conditions, built with locks only.

In conclusion, Call assured Boehm-Bawerk that he would entertain contacts with the ministries involved in the areas of respective competences and would not fail to fulfill Boehm-Bawerk's desire of being notified of the arrangements regarding the initiation of the political *Begehung* and finally, once more suggested clearing the outstanding questions in oral negotiations between the representatives of the two ministries.[31] The real curiosity about Call's letter was that no one reading it at that time, in the summer of 1904, could possibly gauge correctly the real prospects

[31] *Finanzarchiv*, 3120/10.8. Letter of July 24, 1907, bearing the number 434/ G.P.

115

of the canal project in general and of the Danube-Oder Canal in particular. About this, however, more will be said later.

The reaction of the Ministry of Finance to Call's reply was absolutely negative. It was simply noted that the Ministry was unable to agree *to any* aspect of the contents of the Note of the Minister of Commerce, and that no written reply was intended in view of the forthcoming (on August 19, 1904) meeting in conference between Boehm-Bawerk, Koerber, and Call. Prior to that meeting Raymond submitted to his minister a *Pro Memoria* that contained the interesting reference to the "previous question whether any construction should take place at all." In elaboration Raymond dealt with the possible alternatives: (1) a radical one would involve abolition of the Canal Act and its replacement by a River Regulation Act, with the sub-alternative of making use of Article Eleven as soon as the Reichstag should reconvene after the vacation and making action under that article a prerequisite to the beginning of construction; (2) a loyal cooperation in the execution of the Canal Act. At the same time Raymond considered the possibility of a middle road between the two alternatives, that is to say, the continuation of the procrastinating tactics that Raymond (betraying some warmth in the process for which he asked the Minister's forgiveness), argued was inadvisable. It would bring upon the ministry the *odium* of the public, and would only be effective in a very short run. This was in particular true of political *Begehungen*, which were "the first steps toward beginning of construction, in accordance to the law, *although apparently not according to the intentions of Your Excellency.*"[32] The last words quoted clearly implied Boehm-Bawerk's willingness to break the law. Since I have seen it surmised that it was the high financial bureaucracy that opposed the Koerber plan, it should be noted that in the *Pro Memoria* it was Raymond who suggested loyal cooperation in the execution of the Canal Law (thus admitting past lack of loyalty) and advised against continuation of *dilatorische Taktik*.

The ministerial conference on August 19 led to an understand-

---

[32] *Finanzarchiv*, 3130/10.8, August 4, 1904, and same file, August 8, 1904. Italics supplied.

ing, under the terms of which Boehm-Bawerk agreed not to place any further hindrance to the terrain inspection, but did so without prejudice to the definitive approval of the construction proper and reserved the right of possibly making use of Article Eleven of Canal Act. In execution of this understanding, the Ministry agreed to take part in the terrain inspection.

Upon his return from the conference, Boehm-Bawerk wrote out an eight-line instruction to his staff, in execution of which Raymond attached to his *Pro Memoria* "in an envelope a Bill of Law (*Gesetzentwurf*) together with *Motivation* in the matter of carrying out canal constructions."[33]

This envelope remained in the files for sixty-nine years. It was protected by three seals, and across it, in the handwriting of Boehm-Bawerk, were written the words: "May not be opened without permission of the Minister of Finance." On seeing the envelope, I broke Boehm-Bawerk's injunction with the help of my penknife and found inside the draft of a bill composed in the proper form for submittal to the Parliament. The main points of the abortive, but interesting document (the original text of which is reproduced in Appendix Two) were as follows.

Article One of the Bill was intended to amend Article Six of the Canal Law of June 11, 1901, by extending the time when (at the latest) the work on the canals was to begin from 1904 to 1907. This amendment, however, was not to apply to river regulations, work on which would still have to start in 1904. The work on the canals envisaged in Article One of the Canal Law must be completed in 1923 at the latest.

Article Two of the Bill entrusts its execution to the cabinet as a whole.

The very short bill is followed by a brief *Motivation*, which may be quoted *in extenso*:

Apart from difficulties of technical and administrative nature, which militate against beginning construction of waterways still in the current year, the financial condition of the state would not allow at the moment to proceed with the execution of the canal construction program without making special provi-

[33] *Finanzarchiv*, 3130/10.8, September 3, 1904.

sion for the burden of annuities that would emerge from the floatation of the respective loan.

Even though Article Eleven of the Canal Act already contains a provision in this direction, the government, because of the general economic situation, considers the present moment to be altogether unsuitable for presenting such a proposal.

In order to do justice to this point of view and at the same time taking into account the condition of the finances of the state, the government finds a proper solution in the postponement of beginning of construction of waterways, which measure, however, should not extend to the river regulations which in many ways are more urgent and the work on which partly has already begun.

The resolution of the government has been decisively influenced by the consideration that in the immediately following years the market which at present is not very capacious anyhow will be approached by credit operations, designed to provide funds for totally undeferrable purposes to such an extent that the issue of a considerable part of the waterway loan cannot be reasonably thought of.

Since the present bill, as it explicitly emphasizes, is not intended to lead to a postponement of the point of time set for the completion of canal construction, the whole action means merely an abridgement of the period of construction and will therefore lead to a speeding up of construction labors which can be only desirable in the interest of an economical conduct of construction.

Strange indeed that, after a conference in which he reserved the right to have recourse to Article Eleven, Boehm-Bawerk had a bill prepared that rejected such a recourse with an opaque reference to the general economic situation. In a sense, the amending bill was nothing but an attempt to supply a legal cover for the procrastination policy that had been pursued contra-legally for more than three years. Possibly, the calculation was that in 1907 the same methods of obstruction would be used as in 1904. The final point of the *Motivation* regarding the alleged advantages in efficiency gained from foreshortening the period of construction was, of course, blatantly inconsistent with Boehm-Bawerk's violent reaction to Call's proposal for an earlier completion of the program for the first period. This inconsistency does raise a question concerning the intellectual seriousness of the last argument in the *Motivation*. The Bill, incidentally, is silent on what was to happen to the Canal Act's distinction between the two periods of construction and whether additional funds still were, or were not, to be provided after 1912.

But all these points pale into insignificance compared with the instruction to prepare such a Bill behind the back of Koerber, to say nothing of Call. There is no intimation in the files that Boehm-Bawerk had in any way warned his chief of his intention to subvert the Canal Act in this fashion. Boehm-Bawerk's conduct appears, therefore, marred by grave disloyalty. It is true that no practical use was made of this bill. For less than two months after the Bill to amend the Canal Act had been handed to him, Boehm-Bawerk was no longer Minister of Finance. He abandoned his high post on October 26, 1904. Boehm-Bawerk was reported to have said once: "A Minister of Finance must be always ready to resign and [still] must act as though he would never resign."[34] In pursuing his unrelenting struggle against the canals into the last few weeks of his tenure of office, Boehm-Bawerk did act in accordance with the second half of his epigrammatic adage.

The true role of Boehm-Bawerk and his relation to the Koerber experiment have been at times badly distorted in literature. Thus the usually well-informed and accurate Alois Czedik wrote: "However keen he [Boehm-Bawerk] was to increase revenues, he did not raise objections to the great enterprises of projecting a widely spread network of canals, nor to the creation of the Tauern Railroad, nor to the large expansion of the port of Triest. He recognized the high total expenditures as 'productive or competitive' outlays, but believed that because of these plans he would have to assure an increase in budgetary revenues."[35]

---

[34] Joseph Schumpeter, "Eugen von Boehm-Bawerk," *Neue oesterreichische Biographie*, Vienna, 1925, p. 79.

[35] Cf. Alois Czedik, *Zur Geschichte der k.k. oesterreichischen Ministerien, 1861-1916*, Teschen, Vienna, Leipzig, 1920, Vol. III, p. 365.

Three: Stumbling Block

And Schumpeter wrote: "The government, of which he [Boehm-Bawerk] was a member, was based on no [political] party and had to rely on fascinating the public, that is to say, on money spending and great plans which burdened the finances of the State. . . . He acquired from the beginning and maintained in the Cabinet that position which a Minister of Finance in West Europe possesses *ipso facto*, but which must be conquered in Austria. In this case, this was particularly difficult against a Prime Minister, who, full of life as he was, liked to consider himself as the only minister. But Koerber made an exception for Boehm-Bawerk and the two men worked in good agreement with each other. For Koerber knew why he regarded Boehm-Bawerk as a colleague and not as a subordinate, as he was accustomed to do with other ministers. He [Koerber] had won in Boehm-Bawerk not only an international name and an indubitable authority, but also an ideal partner who supported and filled in and complemented the Prime Minister in an excellent fashion. . . . It was to be credited to Boehm-Bawerk that the constructions of railroads, canals, [sic!] and ports, which served the political needs of the government were partly carried through without having the economic achievement compromised by the lack of seriousness regarding the financial bases."[36]

It is true, of course, that railroads had been built and the port facilities in Triest considerably improved, but it is equally true that with regard to Koerber's plans taken as a whole the two statements just quoted are far off the mark. It would have been easy for Schumpeter, the former chief of the Ministry of Finance, to convince himself of the true state of affairs, and so it would have been for Czedik, the indefatigable searcher through archival materials. In the light of the documentation presented in the preceding pages Boehm-Bawerk's actions do not deserve the two admiring tributes.

It gives me no pleasure to be writing these lines. As a young man, I experienced the whole impact of Boehm-Bawerk's analytical powers, particularly of his unbelievable critical acumen in treating the history of doctrines. Nothing can possibly eradicate

[36] Cf. Joseph Schumpeter, "Eugen von Boehm-Bawerk," pp. 79-80.

my feelings of gratitude for an enormous intellectual obligation. But Boehm-Bawerk—a very different Boehm-Bawerk as far as I am concerned—happened to be a crucial figure in the historical events and in the historical problem with which I have become involved. And so I must stifle the private emotions that are trying to stay my pen and honor the truth as I have found it. I do not know whether Boehm-Bawerk, the minister, might have objected, but I am very sure Boehm-Bawerk, the scholar, would have approved.

The Retrospect

IN THE PRECEDING LECTURE the triste story of the canal project was followed as it unfolded. As happens so often, the actual situation was not clear to the contemporaries involved. The Ministry of Commerce—in duty bound—still regarded the canals as a great promise; the Ministry of Finance—in duty derelict—still viewed the canals as a great danger. In reality the canals were neither the one nor the other. As we must change now from story to history, we become aware of the air of unreality that hovered over the whole matter. It is perhaps a testimony to the importance of the canal project that it took so long for the truth to penetrate the skulls of the actors.

Even at the plenary session of the *Beirat*, which at length convened in 1908 after having spent four years in abeyance, no fully frank words were spoken. Baron Fiedler, the new Minister of Commerce, explained the long pause by the difficulties confronted in executing the Canal Act, and still went on to praise the latter as a "bold venture." He added that the funds made available under the act were altogether inadequate and no more than an "advance payment" (*Anzahlung*). Meanwhile, the Minister revealed, the cost estimates had greatly increased, so that the Danube-Oder Canal was calculated to cost about 235 million crowns and the connection to the Vistula River was to require expenditures of about 100 million crowns; total necessary funds, including canalizations in the Elbe basin in Bohemia, it was said, would amount to 370 million crowns. The other projects would be shifted to the "second period of construction." Not a word was said by the Minister about the fact that the explicit provision of the Canal Act (according to which work had to start in 1904 at the latest) had been flagrantly broken.

Nor did the members of the *Beirat* act unduly perturbed by the situation. Rather mildly, they went on to repeat the old arguments in favor of the canals and continued the old exhortations to move

123

from words and studies to deeds.[1] It appears that finally as late as 1910 the plans for the construction of the Danube-Oder Canal were truly ready, projecting 29 locks and two estuaries opposite Vienna (on the left bank of the Danube).[2] But then, in January 1911, Baron Bienerth, the Prime Minister, announced the intention of his government to submit to the Parliament as soon as possible a bill to revise the Canal Act of 1901 "insofar as its execution has proved impossible for technical and financial reasons."[3]

Bienerth's announcement was restated almost verbatim by the Emperor in his throne speech in July 1911 greeting the newly elected Parliament. Indeed, a few months later, on December 19, 1911, the new Prime Minister, Count Stuergkh, submitted a bill to the Parliament designed to "supplement" the Canal Act of 1901. The title of the bill was quite hypocritical because what was being proposed were radical revisions rather than supplements. Nor could the provision of Article One of the bill be taken seriously inasmuch as it proposed a further appropriation of 193 million crowns to be added to the remainder of available funds appropriated earlier, making a total of 310 million crowns. The whole tenor of the bill and of the comments attached to it was extremely restrictive and, in fact, outright negative. The total cost of the 1901 canal project, once said to amount to 750 million crowns, had become, by 1911, 1.2 billion crowns (*Comments*, p. 1) and later even said to require "several billions" (*Comments*, p. 19), the inconsistency remaining unexplained. The bill was to do away with the time limits of the original Canal Bill, envisaging a program for the period 1913–1927, during which work was to be continued and finished on canalizations of rivers in Bohemia and of the Vistula River in Galicia, which still was to be connected with

[1] *Stenographisches Protokoll, Beirat*, Fifth Plenary Session, June 15, 1908.

[2] Ferdinand Lettmayer, ed., *Wien um die Mitte des XX Jahrhunderts*, Vienna, 1958, p. 83.

[3] *Stenographisches Protokoll, Haus der Abgeordneten*, Session XX, *ex* 1917, Meeting 82 (January 17, 1911), p. 4478. Interestingly enough, the Parliament took the announcement with equanimity, except for a big speech by a Social Democratic representative from Galicia who pressed for the canals in order to overcome the economic backwardness of his province and accused the Polish agrarians of having opposed the ambitious project of connecting the Vistula with the Dniester River. (*Ibid.*, pp. 4846-4847.)

the Oder River. For the rest, many rivers were to be regulated, thus meeting the wishes of the agrarians who objected to canals, but favored regulations. The actual canal construction was to be relegated to the years after 1927. The Danube-Oder Canal (still urged in Vienna) would cost now 260 millions and, therefore, was said to be inconsistent with the budgetary situation. Still, one dam and the regulation of the March River along the presumable course of the Danube-Oder Canal were projected for 1913–1927. The Danube-Moldau Canal, which under Koerber was the main instrument of German-Czech reconciliation, was briefly rejected in the *Comments* (p. 20) since there were neither ready technological plans nor available money, and the canal had no economic value anyhow. It was also insisted that long-term plans, embracing decades, were undesirable because the factors involved were liable to change. In particular, the nationalization of railroads since 1904 made canals less desirable, as their lower freight would engender deficits in the operation of state-owned railroads and thus burden the state budget. In short, the "Bill to Supplement"amounted to what is known in Austria as a first class funeral of Koerber's Canal Act of 1901.[4]

The financial history of the Canal Act of 1901 was reported in 1918 in the last months of the Monarchy. It appears that some 50 million crowns had been spent in Bohemia on canalizing the Elbe and Moldau Rivers and some 19 million on canalization of the Vistula River and the Oder-Cracow canal in Galicia, to which another 5 million for a dam in Moravia may be added. All told, from 1904 to 1917, 77 million was expended on actual constructions and an additional 19 million on personnel and overhead costs. Thus of the 250 million (or 229 million effective) that had been appropriated in 1901 for the years 1904–1912, only 96 million, or forty percent, was actually used until 1918. These figures tell the history of a failure in a most drastic language.[5]

Except for some abortive negotiations with Czechoslovakia nothing was done on the Danube-Oder Canal in the interwar

[4] *Stenographisches Protokoll, Haus der Abgeordneten*, Beilagen, Nr. 1087, Session XXI, *ex* 1911.

[5] *Stenographisches Protokoll, Haus der Abgeordneten*, Beilagen, Nr. 1136, Session XXII, *ex* 1918, p. 2.

years; but in October 1939 Hitler's government issued a decree ordering work on the canal to begin. Then, with great energy, men and machines began construction of a port for the canal on the Danube, and three stretches were actually built, amounting in total to 4.6 kilometers (or about 2.8 miles). The war soon stopped the work, and nowadays Viennese living in the vicinity like to use these miniature canals for recreation purposes in the summers, and the relaxed pictures of swimming and sunbathing do not evoke the drama of Koerber's defeat and Boehm-Bawerk's ultimate victory.

As far as Boehm-Bawerk is concerned, an historical retrospect should include a few cogitations that go beyond the description of his froward operations that has been presented in the preceding lecture. Boehm-Bawerk had joined the Ministry of Finance in 1889 when Julian Dunajewski succeeded, after age-long budgetary disorders, to establish a balanced budget. The deed, no doubt, was the prerequisite for Boehm-Bawerk's own work on the reform of direct taxes in the subsequent years. This experience, as well as the traumatic memory of the whole preceding history of the Austrian budget must have been strong upon the mind of Boehm-Bawerk, as it was upon the minds of most Austrian statesmen and the top echelons of the civil service.

Nevertheless, an explanation is not a justification. Least of all can an explanation serve as a vindication when it is grounded in sickly individual and collective memories rather than in the realities of the given historical situation. With regard to the latter, it must be noted that Koerber's advent to power coincided with the end of the mild cyclical upswing that had marked the years 1896–1899. With the year 1900 a wide-spread European depression began, which in Austria lasted until 1905, that is to say throughout the whole period of Koerber's tenure of office. The heavy industry, and notably the iron and steel industry, was affected by the depression with particular force.[6] In the previous discussion of the Koerber experiment a good deal was said about Austria's relative economic backwardness and the country's need

[6] See Emil Bresigar, "Die wirtschaftlichen Konjunktur- und Depressionswellen in Oesterreich seit dem Jahre 1896," *Zeitschrift fuer Volkswirtschaft, Sozialpolitik und Verwaltung*, Vol. 23:1,2 (1914), pp. 1-6, 11, 15.

for accelerated economic development. It was not mentioned, however, that Koerber's experiment also had significant anti-cyclical connotations. The railroad constructions with the attendant increases in rolling stock were bound to reduce unemployment and to aid the ailing heavy industries. In these circumstances, the paranoiac fear of budgetary deficits appears particularly inept. It would never do, however, to reproach Boehm-Bawerk for being blind to Keynesian possibilities more than three decades before the redeeming message was issued. Nor can one criticize Schumpeter, when, in 1925, he published an expansive praise to Boehm-Bawerk's policies of financial orthodoxy.[7] By contrast, a modern economist and a successor of both Boehm-Bawerk and Schumpeter as Austrian Minister of Finance after World War II, is very vulnerable to criticism, when, "without going into details," he once more points to the great desert that he [Boehm-Bawerk] acquired by the fact that, despite the great difficulties of budgetary policy in old Austria, he maintained the balance of the budget and thereby secured the financial stability of the country.[8] Written in the mid-1950s, this is surely a regrettable statement, both from the point of view of economics and economic history.

Yet, leaving aside general theoretical considerations and confining oneself to crude empiricism, Boehm-Bawerk's and his Ministry of Finance policy of fiscal anxiety is difficult to comprehend. In 1902, the year of Koerber's success and his great opportunity, the public debt of Cisleithania amounted to 3,604 million crowns. In 1912, which should have been the last year of "the first period of construction" of canals, the public debt was 7,204 million, having thus risen by 3.5 billion crowns. Military expenditures and the dubious cost of nationalization of railroads were jointly responsible for the doubling of public debt.[9] In the

[7] Joseph Schumpeter, "Eugen von Boehm-Bawerk," p. 79.

[8] Reinhard Kamitz, "Eugen von Boehm-Bawerk," *Neue oesterreichische Biographie ab 1815*, Vol. IX:1, Vienna, 1956, pp. 59-60.

[9] Joseph Puegger, *Fuenfzig Jahre Staatsschuld 1862-1913, Denkschrift aus Anlass des fuenfzigjaehrigen Bestandes einer parlamentarischen Kontrolle der Staatsschuld im Auftrage der Staatsschulden-Kontroll-Kommission des Reichsrates*, Vienna, 1912, p. 567. It is interesting in this connection that Koerber took a strongly negative position against the nationalization of the railroads, which

light of this development, Boehm-Bawerk's penny pinching, "not-one-heller-more-policies," as well as the praise bestowed on him appear to be completely divorced from historical reality. It should be mentioned here that modern economic historians in Austria are beginning to understand the sinister role played and the damage inflicted by fiscal orthodoxy. Thus, Herbert Matis in his extremely brief reference to the Koerber experiment says: "This magistral plan failed—not for the least—because of the resistance of the fiscal thinking of the high ministerial bureaucracy which was primarily interested in the stability of the currency."[10] Similarly, Alois Brusatti makes a general statement: "The predominant weight of financial policy over all economic questions had the result that the economy was essentially viewed as the milch cow of the State. Fiscalism was dominant, that is to say the principle that the State must first and foremost try to fill the Treasury and that considerations of national economic policy were guided by such point of view."[11] It is good that such thoughts begin to acquire recognition in literature. It is another matter that principles, however loudly affirmed, do not necessarily tell the whole story. For one cannot read the files left by Boehm-Bawerk and his staff without receiving the impression that pure departmental interest, the sheer desire to preserve and assert the power of the Ministry of Finance as a value in itself, the "patriotism of office," if not the "insolence of office," ran along among the motivations that guided actions. But this is something that probably is perennially and ubiquitously present in all articulated organizational systems.

---

he claimed threatened "financial ruin" (Josef Redlich, *Schicksalsjahre Oesterreichs 1908-1919*, Graz-Cologne, 1953, Vol. I, p. 29 [November 5, 1909]). It might also be added, that Koerber's former aide Sieghart was very much in favor of the nationalization. (Cf. Rudolf Sieghart, *Die letzten Jahrzehnte einer Grossmacht*, p. 131.)

[10] Cf. Herbert Matis, *Oesterreichs Wirtschaft 1848-1913*, p. 28. Matis's only documentation is a reference to the statement by Spitzmueller that, as previously noted, had directed me to the archive of the Ministry of Finance. Hence Matis's reference to "high bureaucracy" and his failure to mention Boehm-Bawerk.

[11] Alois Brusatti, *Oesterreichische Wirtschaftspolitik vom Josephinismus zum Staendestatt*, Vienna, 1965, p. 77.

Four: Retrospect

The remainder of this lecture will deal with three related sub-jects. First, there will be a review of the way in which Koerber has been treated in literature, both by historians and by contem-poraries in their memoirs and diaries. Then something will be said about the two or so last years of Koerber's tenure of office, the period of his decline and fall. Finally, a summarizing appraisal of the man and his "era" will be attempted. It is neither very easy nor uniformly pleasant to scrutinize the writings that have been devoted to Koerber. As Schiller said of his Wallenstein, "con-fused by the parties' favor and hatred, the image of his character fluctuates in history." Indeed, long grudges originating in de-ceived ambitions, political biases that strangely survived in full vigor the turbulence of the intervening historical changes, the bu-reaucrats' dislikes of a routine-destroying innovator—all these with some admixture of reluctant praise and a few frankly positive appraisals characterize the bulk of relevant literature.

Among the political biases, the voice of political Catholicism rings out with particular clarity. Herwig Leitgeb, while working on his Ph.D. thesis on Koerber, had an interview with the aged Spitzmueller in which the latter told the young man inter alia: "Von Koerber was *innerly* very anti-clerical. Yet in view of the strictly Catholic Imperial House, he knew how to conceal his po-sition carefully, because frankness in this respect could do him nothing but harm."[12]

Neither Spitzmueller nor anyone else, of course, knew what was going on in the innermost recesses of Koerber's soul. It is true, however, that throughout Koerber's period in office, the country was somewhat disturbed by the "Away from Rome" (*Los from Rom*) movement that had been initiated by the radical pan-Germans and sought to bring about conversions from Catholicism to Lutheranism. In the face of demands to use police against the movement, Koerber replied that too much police action was a dubious matter under all conditions; that the movement, if left alone, would soon run its course; and, finally, that the Catholic

[12] Herwig Leitgeb, "Die Ministerpraesidentshaft Dr. Ernest von Koerbers . . . ," p. 67. Interview with Baron Spitzmueller on March 5, 1953. Italics supplied.

Church in Austria in its strength was perfectly able to take care of itself.[13] It appears that Koerber was able to induce both the reluctant Emperor and at least two high dignitaries of the Church to accept the wisdom of his position.[14] It seems, however, that the representatives of political Catholicism never quite reconciled themselves to that tolerant policy. In general it must be admitted that there were aspects of Koerber's policies that in a very general and subtle way connected him with the Josephinism of the eighteenth century that brought Austria the *Toleranz Patent* of 1781, a modern measure of fundamental importance, even though complete equality of Protestants was not achieved until eighty years later.

Let us see first, in this connection, how Koerber and his period in office is judged by Hugo Hantsch, a frankly Catholic historian who, after World War II, held the chair in Austrian history at the University of Vienna. Having described briefly the short period of eager parliamentary activity, Hantsch refers to the return of obstruction in the Parliament, which he explains by "the doctrine having been stronger than reason" and by "the egotism of the parties which stifled all reasonable will." The term "party egotism" was an essential element in the political lingo of the reactionaries in the First Austrian Republic when they were engaged in struggles that ended with the destruction of the democratic constitution, the abolition of all political parties, and the establishment of the regime of Catholic fascism in the country.[15] Professor Hantsch seems to know nothing of the obstruction within the cabinet to which Koerber's program was exposed; what Matis and Brusatti know or suspect now was entirely beyond his purview. Nor is Hantsch in the least interested in the problems of that economic program; there is no understanding of the opportunities that were open to Koerber upon his triumphs.

Hantsch's actual appraisal reads as follows: "In the course of

---

[13] Gustav Kolmer, *Parlament und Verfassung in Oesterreich*, Vol. VIII, pp. 217-218.

[14] Josef Redlich, *Schicksalsjahre*, Vol. I, p. 28 (November 5, 1909).

[15] It is not surprising, therefore, that in another publication Professor Hantsch presents a staunch defense of Chancellor Dollfuss, the engineer of the brazen breach of the constitution.

time the governmental activity of von Koerber has been judged in very contradictory terms. Precisely because the beginning was so very promising, the subsequent judgments were so detracting. Koerber was reproached, probably justly, because he had not seriously attacked any of the decisive problems, but was much too concerned with superficial success. He wanted to rule Austria bureaucratically, without considering that he did not have at his disposal the power which [after the revolution of 1848] was in the hands of Bach and Bruck. Koerber started, it was said, enterprises that were neither theoretically prepared nor could they be financed. Koerber was further said to have favored pushing ambitions (*Streberei*), was not miserly with various honors and distinctions and in particular failed to draw a clear line between the Government and the high treason of extreme radicalism." Hantsch follows this bouquet with two uncited quotations, one of rather sharp, if not coarse, strictures and the other very positive by Charmatz, to which Hantsch adds that "forty years" earlier, however, Charmatz did not judge so favorably when he wrote: "He [Koerber] left the office, and the conditions he left behind were more confused than they had been when he arrived at power."[16] There will be presently an opportunity to refer further to Charmatz's views.

A symposium about "men who had formed the destinies of Austria," edited by Hantsch, includes a paper on Koerber by Professor Alexander Novotny, a man closely allied spiritually to Hantsch. Novotny like Hantsch is an exclusively political historian and as such really unqualified to write about Koerber. Accordingly his paper contains no more than the briefest factual reference to Koerber's economic program. Instead, "in order to characterize Koerber as a man of economic policies," there is a description of his negotiations with the Hungarians about the controversial railroads in Bosnia. For the rest, the paper deals with political problems that Koerber faced and finally arrives at an attempt at personal characterization, the cloven foot finally appearing in a slur on Koerber's private life:

[16] Hugo Hantsch, *Die Geschichte Oesterreichs*, Vol. II, Vienna, 1955, pp. 482, 484-485.

Four: Retrospect

"There are few personalities in the history of Austria with regard to whom the question whether we have to do with a great statesman is so difficult to decide as it is precisely in the case of Koerber. The fact that he became prime minister as head of a civil service cabinet at a most difficult time; that he was the first head of government in Austrian history who did not belong to the high nobility, but was a *'Herr von'* brought him sympathies from diverse sides. Later he was judged less favorably. Koerber was certainly an important personality, and even his exterior was interesting. He did not have the clear-cut profile of a Roman, nor the fine aristocratic veneer [?] of the *Biedermeier* period. . . . Men who had listened to him as a speaker relate even today that Koerber, when he remained silent, made a very ordinary, petty-bourgeois impression. Even the expression 'a Bohemian cobbler' was once used. But it was also said that *all* these disadvantageous things were *fully* overlooked when one listened to one of his brilliant speeches that at times could even carry away. Koerber was a strong spirit oriented to a definite end. The office, the files, the economic and administrative problems filled him entirely. His activity in the Academy of Sciences testifies to some interest in the sciences. He had apparently no interest at all for theater, art, and literature. He loved to be instructed about world and man not by books but by the files and life itself.

"After the strenuous work in the office he sought relaxation in his relation to the wife of a Vienna lawyer which hardly can be called platonic. A number of older ladies and gentlemen still remember today the conspicuous red-headed lady—not precisely a classic beauty, but very interesting; she was said to be very intelligent and witty. For many years Koerber appeared with her regularly on the *Semmering*, [a well known Alpine resort near Vienna] and elsewhere in public. One may try as a Christian to extend forgiving understanding to the weakness of others. But as a historian one must declare: This is a sign of heavy decadence. One cannot imagine that anything of this sort would have been possible at the time of Austria's rise to the position of Great Power."

132

Four: Retrospect

This incoherent passage with its arrogance of class and nationality—the offensive reference to the Czechs—ending in a bit of shamefully coarse gossip and inane general cogitations, reveals a depth of hostility to Koerber that cannot be understood except as being politically motivated. It may also be noted that the same volume contains two other contributions from Novotny's pen, one on the Emperor Francis Joseph and the other on Metternich. It is interesting to see that in dealing with the Emperor's relation to Frau Schratt, Novotny finds the proper gentlemanly tone without speculations about the nature of the relationship; and writing about Metternich he refers to the man's promiscuity in the tenderly phrased sentence: "Metternich's private life was not such as to appear dominated by the moral law of Christianity."[17]

For the sake of contrast, it may be in order to show how a gentleman refers to Koerber's private relationship. After having mentioned Koerber's rather lonely death (in 1919) in a sanitarium in a little town near Vienna, the writer says: "There were no relatives present. Only a lady whom he [Koerber] had admired for a long time, came from Vienna. Visibly most deeply stirred, she made the arrangements for the funeral with great care and deliberation. Her still obvious great beauty and the faithfulness with which she stood by Koerber in his death did justify the warm feelings which he had devoted to her during his life."[18]

It is, of course, not very useful to raise the question whether someone was or was not "a great statesman" without revealing the criteria by which "greatness" is to be measured. But in fairness to Novotny, it must be said that as an afterthought he comes close to giving such a criterion. He writes: "We want to add that what Koerber lacked to be a great statesman was not a want of abilities, but of an attitude of the soul that did not have the force to do calmly, surely, smilingly, with iron nerves, and full of *faithful* assurance what was inevitably necessary and the only right thing.

---

[17] Hugo Hantsch, ed., *Gestalter der Geschicke Oesterreichs*, Vienna-Munich, 1962: Alexander Novotny, "Ministerpraesident Ernest von Koerber," p. 496; and "Kaiser Franz Joseph 1," p. 442; and "Staatskanzler Clemens Wenzel Fuerst Metternich," pp. 340-341.

[18] Cf. Robert Ehrhart, *Im Dienste des alten Oesterreich*, p. 363.

Four: Retrospect

One cannot eschew the impression that much, in fact everything done by Koerber was done because of the effect, because of the façade that had to be built, regardless of whether this was to lead to a definitive or only to a temporary cure of conditions."[19]

Thus, we have been provided with a simple method by which a great statesman can be unerringly recognized. This chitchat could be disregarded, except for the telling reference to "faithful assurance." For Novotny is by no means alone in charging Koerber with a lack of faith. Friedrich Funder, who for long decades was the editor-in-chief of the Viennese organ of the Catholic Christian Social Party, writes about Koerber: "Coming from the liberal school, a skeptic for whom there were *no immutable values*, he placed in his calculations the egotism of [political] parties as the most important factor."[20] Very similarly Spitzmueller pronounces: "Koerber had no truly creative concept. His gift of sharp criticism, together with a far-reaching skepticism, often proved harmful in an Empire, in whose future one had to have *faith* in order to achieve something."[21] The question of the allegedly lacking faith apart, it is curious on the part of Spitzmueller who, as we know, had confessed, if not boasted, of having undermined Koerber's very creative program, to accuse Koerber of not possessing a "creative concept." But political bias in general stands high above the pedantic precept of consistency.

The adverse judgments just quoted—all of them published after World War II—are, however, less negative than some of the contemporary opinions that are burdened by petty personal resent-

[19] Alexander Novotny, "Ernest von Koerber," p. 499. Italics supplied.

[20] Friedrich Funder, *Vom Gestern ins heute*, Vienna, 1952, p. 231. Italics supplied.

[21] Alexander Spitzmueller, . . . *und hat auch Ursach*, p. 46. Italics supplied. The Christian Social Party of the period had in its fairly forward ranks a parliamentarian, a certain Bielohlawek, who acquired considerable renown by a number of odd aphorisms. One of them was: "When I hear of a book, I should like to puke." Another was, "I know all about scholarship. That is what one Jew cribs from another." Cribbing or no cribbing, this uniformity in the appraisals of Koerber does reveal the sameness of a political bias. Incidentally, it may be noted that no one raises in the same tone the same charge of lack of faith against Boehm-Bawerk who, with regard to the deteriorating relations between Austria and Hungary, was reported to have said that he "sensed the iron step of history pointing toward dissolution of Austria-Hungary." *Ibid.*, p. 59.

ments, initiated by momentary political anger, and characterized by animosity toward liberal reforming policies. This is especially true of the diary of Joseph Maria Baernreither, a leading German parliamentarian (as such a member of the party of "Constitution-faithful Large-Estate-Owners"), who, in 1898 under Thun, had briefly been Minister of Commerce, was valued for his considerable erudition in economic matters, and withal was very much a liberal conservative—the oxymoron making very good sense on the parliamentary scene in Austria in the last decades of the past century. Leitgeb, in his Ph.D. thesis, praises Baernreither's judgments of Koerber as "intelligent" and "very objective."[22] We shall have an opportunity to see how far this objectivity extended.

Like everybody else, Baernreither cannot help mentioning Koerber's industry, conscientiousness, knowledgeability, reservation, and circumspection, which he regards as "great" while describing Koerber's ability to make decisions and his energy as "small."[23] After this praise, immediately interspersed with abusive little personal remarks (p. 120), Baernreither went on to describe "the infinite tenacity" with which Koerber negotiated the canal project that became "the pivot of his policy" (p. 122). Baernreither supported the canal project "to make the best of it," even though he regarded much of it as "utopian." His main objection, however, was political. In this respect, he said, Koerber had miscalculated altogether by "buying at much too high prices." The reference is to concessions to the Czechs that Koerber made in order to facilitate the passing of his investment bills. The "too high prices" consisted of the government's subvention of 16 million crowns for the improvement of the sewage system in Prague, of the agreement to establish there a privately financed Modern Art Gallery, and finally, of arranging of the Emperor's journey to Prague for the dedication of a new bridge over the Moldau

[22] Herwig Leitgeb, "Die Ministerpraesidentshaft Dr. Ernest von Koerber," p. II.

[23] Joseph Maria Baernreither, *Der Verfall des Habsburgerreiches und die Deutschen, Fragmente eines politischen Tagebuches, 1897-1917*, Oskar Mitis, ed., Vienna, 1938, pp. 116, 119. In the following, the pages of the diary are cited in the text in parentheses.

135

River.[24] The Emperor's travel expenses are nowhere given, but clearly it betrayed neither intelligence nor objectivity to regard these trifles as a "high price" for the cessation of parliamentary obstruction and the adoption of the investment bills.

The main thrust of Baernreither's strictures, however, was directed elsewhere. He disliked Koerber's Press Bill, which he said was designed "to win the press" (p. 128), and even more his policies toward the press to which he gave information and indiscretions of all kinds, the whole press policy having been "totally demoralizing." "Journalists of all parties admitted openly that they supported Koerber because he favored their specific journalistic interests." "The Parliament was left aside. He had less and less contact with deputies, and caused all independent thinking to be persecuted" (p. 137). In view of the well-known facts to the contrary, the last remark smacks of persecution mania and personal resentment. Nor is it very consistent with the statement "that he [Koerber] had admirers among the parliamentarians and particularly among the aristocrats remains a *testimonium paupertatis* for these circles. The secret was that everybody found his profit. Koerber gave freely out orders and elevations to nobility. The press had a perfectly free hand, and freedom of assembly was unrestricted" (p. 138). During a trip by Baernreither in Bohemia, he discovered that a public school principal in a little town was to give a lecture on "a socialist topic of the day." Baernreither went to the district chief to denounce the act, but the latter was told by the Governor of Bohemia (Koerber's subordinate) not to interfere (p. 138). Koerber even talked to the leaders of the Social Democratic Party, with whom, as another writer reported, his relations were "directly those of friendship" (*geradezu freundschaftlich*).[25]

Description of these horrors reveals the strength of antidemocratic beliefs within the so-called liberal German bourgeoisie (*Buergertum*) of the period. But ideas apart, it is Baernreither's personal hostility to Koerber that stands out and makes him accuse the Prime Minister of lying: "A deep trait of untruth-

[24] *Ibid.*, p. 123. Gustav Kolmer, *Parlament und Verfassung*, Vol. VIII, pp. 197, 304.

[25] Joseph Redlich, *Kaiser Franz Joseph von Oesterreich*, Berlin, 1929, p. 398.

fulness characterized his method. . . . It is certain that in his oral dealings he *sometimes* deviated from the truth in a serious (*bedenklich*) way" (p. 141). At one point, Baernreither even told Joseph Redlich: "He [Koerber] has cheated everybody."[26] All this did not prevent Baernreither earlier in his *Diary* from going out of his way to praise Koerber's honesty (p. 58). Spitzmueller, blowing into the same horn and telling young Leitgeb in an interview things he had hesitated to print in his memoirs, explained that Koerber would have considered excessive love of truth, unless it brought him real advantages, as "political dilettantism."[27] Leitgeb, unwilling to see the hero of his thesis blackened too much, adds a not untypical excuse: Koerber, "however, was doubtless influenced to a certain degree by his Chief of the Presidial Chancellery (*Praesidialkanzlei*) Rudolf Sieghart, . . . a Jew and a fairly gifted brain" (*ibid*).

It has been customary in the literature to complain of the "corrupt practices" of Koerber's administration, be they Christian or Jewish. There is little doubt that a secret "disposition fund" existed, financed largely from contributions of ambitious people anxious to acquire honorific titles and orders, including perhaps membership in the First Chamber of the Parliament. To some extent the fund was used to satisfy journalists and perhaps certain members of the Second Chamber. Joseph Redlich speaks in this connection of the deep depravity of the Austrian Parliament that was brought about thereby and of the "fine poison of corruption which deeply penetrated the whole State and all its nationalities."[28] With regard to the alleged press corruption, Heinrich Friedjung, in his biographical paper on Koerber, very reasonably suggests that monetary subventions alone would not have assured Koerber of support by the press; Koerber's predecessors such as Taaffe and Badeni were by no means stingy in this respect and yet they could not assure for themselves a friendly press. By contrast, Friedjung says, Koerber's success depended essentially on the full

[26] Joseph Redlich, *Schicksalsjahre*, Vol. II, p. 151.

[27] Herwig Leitgeb, "Die Ministerpraesidentshaft Dr. Ernest von Koerbers," p. 113.

[28] Joseph Redlich, *Kaiser Franz Joseph*, pp. 397-398.

freedom which he accorded to the press and tolerated the newspapers' criticism of his policies.[29]

The relations of the Prime Minister with the press were clearly built upon mutual confidence, and the main trouble was that Koerber's recourse to public opinion was neither understood nor appreciated by men raised in the traditions of the Austrian *Obrigkeitsstaat*. Only within the framework of these ugly traditions can one take the oft-repeated statement that Koerber ruled with the press against the Parliament.[30]

With regard to Koerber's relations with the members of Parliament, far from ignoring the Parliament, Koerber's innovation consisted in descending from the Olympian heights on which his predecessors had resided and becoming accessible to the deputies. The latter could come to him with the manifold pressing problems of their constituencies, which is something that is regarded as normal function of parliamentarians in Anglo-Saxon democracies. It is probable that in this connection some extra-legal favors were dispensed, but some of the quid-pro-quo was received by Koerber in terms of support in the Parliament and of information on the attitudes and planned moves of the political parties. At any rate, this was the very opposite of neglect of Parliament, and it is little short of ridiculous to level such a charge against the man who had awakened the Parliament from the years of its nightmarish sleep.[31]

[29] Heinrich Friedjung, "Ernest von Koerber," *Neue oesterreichische Biographie*, Vol. I, pp. 28-29.

[30] This is thoughtlessly repeated even by Mommsen, who ought to have known better. Hans Mommsen, *Die Sozialdemokratie*, p. 347.

[31] It might also be added that there is a good deal of hypocrisy about all the talk about sale of titles, etc., with which Koerber allegedly marred the pristine purity of the Austrian government. A little story involving no other than the Emperor Francis Joseph, that paragon of duty and integrity, should help to put things into perspective: The daughter of a rich contractor, a commoner, was to marry a scion of high nobility, and it seemed desirable to the father of the bride to disguise the misalliance by having nobility rank bestowed upon himself. At the same time Wittek, then Minister of Commerce, was interested in obtaining half-a-million crowns for the financing of a politically important local railroad and wanted to "squeeze" the amount out of the man in exchange for his elevation to the rank. When the matter was presented to the Emperor, his resolution was: "Let Wittek go on squeezing," whereupon the deal was closed to the satisfaction of both parties. Cf. Erich Graf Kielmansegg, *Kaiserhaus, Staatsmaenner und Politiker*, p. 50.

Four: Retrospect

Some of the adverse criticisms, other reasons apart, derive clearly from grudges of people who at some point did not find Koerber amenable to their own ambitions. To some extent, this shimmers through in Baernreither's *Diary*. But both Spitzmueller and Redlich very much deserve to be mentioned in this connection; neither man received an appointment as Minister of Finance in October 1916, when Koerber, who had become Prime Minister for the second time, was selecting the members of his cabinet. Spitzmueller wrote frankly: "I confess quite openly that I expected with certainty that Koerber would invite me to become the Minister of Finance in his government."[32] Redlich describes his conversation with Koerber on the same subject in his *Diary*. The entry is angry and abusive, accusing Koerber of crass vanity, mendacity, and histrionics.[33] It should be noted that neither man had received from Koerber any previous hint, let alone a promise, regarding a role in the cabinet. Nevertheless, Leitgeb happily pronounces that "Spitzmueller, too, was deceived by Koerber." He hastens to add that this fact could not detract from Spitzmueller's objectivity [in the interview on Koerber] and goes on to praise Spitzmueller's mature judgment, calmed by age (*abgeklaert*), which is not a very plausible statement in view of the rather negative pronouncements in that interview.[34] Be it political bias or personal grudges, surely resentments of this kind must be discounted when reading the literature on Koerber, which unfortunately means only that it is advisable to keep them in mind.

Two more references should be mentioned before finishing this survey of the unfavorable appraisals. Erich Graf Kielmansegg, who (with a short interruption) was the Governor of Lower Austria (which then included Vienna) from 1889 to 1911, may be regarded—despite his non-Austrian origins—in his *Weltanschauung* as the true emanation of the old Austrian bureaucracy. It is, therefore, not surprising that, in dealing with Koerber, he places central emphasis on what he sees as the deterioration in the standards and in the power of bureaucracy. It is probably quite true that in his policy of appointing civil servants

[32] Alexander Spitzmueller, . . . *und hat auch Ursach*, p. 171.

[33] Josef Redlich, *Schicksalsjahre*, Vol. II, pp. 150-151 (October 28, 1916).

[34] Herwig Leitgeb, "Die Ministerpraesidentshaft Dr. Ernest von Koerbers," p. IV.

Koerber kept account of the wishes of the individual parliamentarians who tried to push their protégés.[35] What escaped Kielmansegg altogether was that Koerber was engaged in a change of the social complexion of the higher ranks of ministerial bureaucracy. Noble descent was no longer sufficient to assure a high position in the hierarchy. If Karl Renner, writing in 1908, could claim that "our bureaucracy is a branch of the bourgeoisie," this to a large extent was a rather recent phenomenon, largely originated in the years of Koerber's tenure of office.[36]

Finally, there was Baron Plener, a leader of the liberal Germans in the Parliament, who combined considerable erudition with great interest in economic problems. Nevertheless, in his memoirs he hardly touched on Koerber's main idea, except for describing Koerber's opinion that a program of investments in railroads and canals would deflect the deputies from national strife as somewhat gullible (*vertrauensselig*); and for deploring the great financial outlays "which essentially had the *only* purpose of appeasing the refractory opposition in the Parliament."[37] Very similarly, also for Kielmansegg "the Canal Act of 1901 had the *only* purpose to win for the Government the votes of deputies and speculators."[38]

The nearly verbatim accord in the opinions of Plener and Kielmansegg is not without interest, although it probably derived from different motivations. Kielmansegg, interested as he was in the functioning of bureaucracy, had little interest, in economic problems while the economically educated Plener, the liberal, was distrustful of governmental interventions in the field of economy. Both men, as so many others, failed to understand that Koerber's program had a value, quite independent from the political effects of the moment.

Lest the preceding survey appear one-sided, it should be said that nearly everybody writing about Koerber, including his most acrimonious critics, could not help bestowing some praise on the man. Thus, Hantsch spoke of the "grandeur and wealth of ideas"

[35] Erich Graf Kielmansegg, *Kaiserhaus*, pp. 291, 295.

[36] Karl Renner, *Der nationale Streit um die Aemter und die Sozialdemokratie*, Vienna, 1908, p. 7.

[37] Ernst Freiherr von Plener, *Erinnerungen*, Stuttgart and Leipzig, 1921, Vol. III, pp. 317, 323, and 328-329. Italics supplied.

[38] Erich Graf Kielmansegg, *Kaiserhaus*, p. 291. Italics supplied.

in Koerber's program; Novotny of Koerber's "knowledge and experience." Spitzmueller regarded Koerber as "the most outstanding personality within the hierarchy of the Austrian civil service." Baernreither mentioned Koerber's "great intelligence" (although along with a "lack of political character"); and Redlich, in an unguarded moment, even referred to Koerber's "political genius," while Funder praised Koerber's "universal knowledge" and brilliance as an expert in government administration.[39] The only trouble is that the praising phrases, lightly dropped from the end of the pen, are submerged in the flood of expressions of disapproval and accusations.

In fact, apart from Baron Czedik's insightful treatment, to which reference will be made below, it is only in Richard Charmatz's little piece that the distribution of approval and disapproval is reversed and the negative features almost disappear in the general recognition of Koerber's achievements. For Charmatz, Koerber was above all a great modernizer, and Charmatz's article bears the banner-like title "A Modern Prime Minister, Ernest von Koerber." Let me say at once that even Charmatz, concerned as he is with modernization, devotes just a few lines to Koerber's economic project and has not a word to spare about Koerber's attempt to modernize the economy of Cisleithania. It seems that a political historian in Austria is almost professionally barred from encompassing problems of economic history within his purview. Thus for Charmatz, Koerber's modernity lay essentially in the field of political or rather administrative activity. On that point Charmatz is outspoken: Koerber's "whole being radiated modernity, he had a feeling for the step of time, and was by no means willing to treat with reverence the legacy of the past, the tradition."[40] Here is what Charmatz essentially means by Koerber as a "modernizer":

---

[39] Hugo Hantsch, *Geschichte Oesterreichs*, Vol. II, p. 482; Alexander Novotny, "Ernest von Koerber," p. 487; Alexander Spitzmueller, . . . *und hat auch Ursach*, p. 125; Friedrich Funder, *Von Gestern ins heute*, p. 231; Josef Redlich, "Introduction" to J. M. Baernreither, *Fragments of a Political Diary*, London, 1930, p. xxii.

[40] Richard Charmatz, *Lebensbilder aus der Geschichte Oesterreichs*, Vienna, 1947, "Ein moderner Ministerpraesident, Dr. Ernest von Koerber," p. 165. Further citation to pages of this article will be given in the text in parentheses.

Four: Retrospect

"If Dr. von Koerber saw that the Parliament left him in the lurch in his modern and modernizing endeavors, he strove all the more eagerly to assure for the population a full enjoyment of civil rights and to redeem it from the burden of paternalization [by the authorities]. Never before had the press in Austria been so free of all censorship and other harassments as it was under this Prime Minister. The press could really move without let and hindrance within legal limits. It could criticize when necessary and do so to its heart's content. Similarly, freedom of assembly and freedom of speech became undiluted truths. Everybody was allowed to say what he innerly felt impelled to. He did not have to fear the obnoxious supervision by civil servants who at times were stupid men and not in line with the times (*zeitfremd*). Also the whole administrative apparatus received a generous greasing, some of its rusty wheels were exchanged, and its mode of operation was fundamentally revised. No excessive paperwork, no waste of time, no impediments of the economy or of the cultural development! Instead a reasonable and benevolent concern with the wishes and the needs of the population. A general administrative reform was planned, without, however, evolving beyond the drafting stage. Nor did justice escape the renovation. Koerber was not only Prime Minister and Minister of the Interior, but for some time he also was Minister of Justice. As such he admonished the judges to be impartial in applying the law. He urged upon them a libertarian interpretation of the Press Law, particularly since the plan to create a new press law never could reach full maturity. It is true, that because of the failure of the Parliament that tore itself asunder, the position of bureaucracy was particularly strong. But the civil service was trained to avoid any inane bureaucratism (pp. 170-171)."

Charmatz also devotes a passage to Koerber's relation to labor, to the social problem, to the Social Democracy which was entitled to approval by all men of equitable thinking. In this connection he mentions the reasonable settlement of the miners' strike in Bohemia and the eventual reduction of the working day in the mines to nine hours. He also mentions Koerber's bill for old age insurance. "As a matter of course were stopped," Charmatz says, "the dumb, brazen, and petty everyday harassments which the Viennese *Arbeiter-Zeitung* for such a long time used to register in its column: 'How we are Being Treated.' The new tone reminded the people that a new time of social understanding had come for the world and, by the same token, also for Austria" (pp. 173-174).

In conclusion, Charmatz, too, raises the popular question whether Koerber was "a great statesman." But, unlike Novotny in the previously quoted passage, Charmatz avoids meaningless flapdoodle. He thinks in historical terms. His answer is "no," in the sense that Koerber does not belong to the group that comprises Washington, Pitt, Disraeli, Cavour. "But it may be said," he continues, "that Koerber was a great Austrian Prime Minister" (p. 176). Thus he arrives at his concluding sentence: "Koerber had renovated Austria in her spirit by introducing, wherever he could, modern (*zeitfrische*) methods into the public administration" (*ibid.*).

Charmatz's appraisal of Koerber has a "modern" sound in our time when "modernity" and "modernization" have become popular terms that appear in the titles of numerous articles and books claiming scholarly recognition and value. The trouble is that the claims are just as ill-founded as they are broad and sweeping. C. E. Black, for instance, does not hesitate to assert that "for the first time in history a universal pattern of modernity is emerging."[41]

Despite all the printing ink spent, the truth is that the concept of modernization remains highly uncertain. "Disputable," "loose," "vague," "general," "ambiguous," "amorphous" are the terms used in describing the concept of modernization.[42] Wehler has written a serious and thoughtful book. His attitude is

[41] See Cyril Edwin Black, "Change as a Condition of Modern Life" in Myron Weiner, ed., *Modernization: The Dynamics of Growth*, New York-London, 1966, p. 17.

[42] Cf. e.g., E. A. Wrigley, "The Process of Modernization and Industrial Revolution in England," *Journal of Interdisciplinary History*, Vol. 3, 1972/73, p. 225; Myron Weiner, *Modernization*, p. v; Hans-Ulrich Wehler, *Modernisierung und Geschichte*, Goettingen, 1975, p. 11.

critical, and at times he raises the question whether the concept should not be abandoned altogether, although he also realizes that scholarly strictures are fairly powerless against a *"Modewort,"* a term of popular fashion.[43] Other less scrupulous scholars, although mentioning the deficiencies of the concept, go on using it *medén diakrinómenos*.[44] When it comes to the laborious search for a clear definition, one author offers as a summary the following definition of modernization: "In short, all these definitions emphasize new ways of thinking which make it possible for men to create *modern* industries, *modern* society, and *modern* government."[45] It is hardly possible to beg a question in a more unabashed fashion.

The conceptual mess becomes particularly visible once people stop identifying modernization with "Westernization," "Europeanization," or even "civilization" *tout court*, and begin to speak of a "universal pattern of modernity" (*vide supra*). Then anything goes: introducing a bill of civil rights and making its execution practicable is "modern." But then a totalitarian dictatorship where all those rights, such as freedom of speech, press and assembly, are ruthlessly denied is also "modern." An agrarian reform that gives land to the peasantry is "modern," but so is also a collectivization that takes land away from the peasantry. *Bastille* was not "modern" at all, but concentration camps are. Breaking modern machinery as the Luddites did was not modern, but now every self-respecting student devours the book by E. P. Thompson,[46] where the Luddites appear as the cradle of the modern labor movement. Genghis Khan was not modern, but a "Genghis Khan with a telephone," to use Tolstoy's phrase, or even with an atomic bomb, is very modern indeed in that universal, ubiquitous concept of modernity where "recentness" has come to equal "modernity."

The point is that it makes some sense to speak of "modernity" in two respects. First, when we deal with a clearly measurable increase in speed, efficiency, productivity. Thus a steam engine was

---

[43] *Ibid.*, p. 44.

[44] "Nothing wavering," as St. James used to say, *Epistle* I:6.

[45] Myron Weiner, *Modernization*, "Introduction," p. 4. Italics supplied.

[46] *The Making of the English Working Class*, London, 1965.

indeed more modern than a windmill or even the watermill; a railroad was more modern than a bullock cart; a jet plane is more modern than a propeller-driven plane. In such cases of unidirectional evolution involving technology and know-how, one knows clearly what one means. Similarly, the situation is obvious with increase in literacy, but when it comes to literature, who dares say whether Ionesco, Beckett, Pinter, and *tutti quanti* are more modern than Shakespeare, even though they are more recent?

Second, it can be meaningful to speak of modernity and modernization once the question is placed within a clearly determined historical pattern. But the historical and geographic pattern must be narrowly and intelligibly defined.[47] This consideration brings us at length back to Charmatz and his appraisal of Koerber. Charmatz's view cannot be faulted precisely because he moves within an intelligible historical comparison. What he has in mind is the traditional Austrian absolutism, what in Austria is called the "pre-March" (*Vormaerz*) period, referring to Metternich, the previously mentioned "*Obrigkeitsstaat*," and to a political and social system with a strong predominance of aristocracy, that is to say, of ascribed status over achieved status. At the same time, though more vaguely, "the ideas of 1789" serve to round off the *tertium comparationis*. In this sense, we know exactly why Charmatz calls Koerber modern and speaks of his modernity when he refers to Koerber's emphasis on reducing the willful arbitrary activities of bureaucracy, police, and courts, and to his transformation of the constitutionally stipulated bill of rights into the reality of everyday life of the citizens of the country, and to radical changes of the policies governing the recruitment of bureaucracy.

Yet Charmatz can be criticized not for what he says but for what he does not say. His failure properly to emphasize Koerber's

---

[47] Therefore, when S. N. Eisenstadt (*Modernization: Protest and Change*, Englewood Cliffs, N.J., 1966) speaks of the "First Phase of Modernization" and of the "Second Phase of Modernization" (the latter including present-day totalitarian societies), he pretends to be historical, but I still do not know what he is talking about, particularly when he informs me that "modern societies are in some sense [?] democratic" (p. 4).

contribution to economic history is regrettable precisely in the connection under review here. At one point, Wehler says: "Many theorists see the main advantage of the modernization process . . . in the growing power of man over his natural and social environment."[48] This *is* economic development in general and industrialization in particular, for which clear concepts no ambiguous term is necessary. In trying to launch a spurt of economic development and in building the infra-structure to support it, Koerber certainly was a great "modernizer" in both reasonable meanings of the term. But industrialization in backward countries of Europe in the nineteenth and early twentieth centuries involved novelty in a different and more specific historical sense. Being deprived by the very virtue of its backwardness of factors of development that had served as "preconditions" or "prerequisites" in more advanced countries, a backward country in its process of industrialization developed devices that could be used as a "substitute" for the missing prerequisites. In this sense, Koerber's idea to use the government's investment program as the vehicle of economic development in Austria was precisely a novelty, and, if one insists on using the term, an attempt at "modernization" within the historical pattern of European industrializations.

It is regrettable that Charmatz misses this point altogether. On the other hand, what Charmatz has to say about Koerber's attitude to the Austrian labor movement and to measures of legislative social policy, such as old age insurance, clearly derived from the preceding industrialization of the country. Such measures and the spirit behind them were to become more and more important, as industrialization went on and the industrial labor force and the workers' claims upon protection by the state were going to increase *pari passu* with the growth of factories and increases in industrial output.

As said before, the crucial moment for Koerber was the summer of 1902, when, at the acme of success, he ought to have re-initiated the policy of the great spurt. Once the right moment was missed, nothing could follow but a protracted period of decline that lasted for another two and a half years until Koerber's fall at the very end of 1904. It should not take long to summarize the

[48] Wehler, *Modernisierung*, p. 17.

history of those rather melancholy thirty months. The reaction to the failure was quick, and perhaps not surprisingly so. As early as September 1902 there began rumors in parliamentary circles about renewal of Czech obstruction and possible dissolution of the Parliament. After a couple of years during which the language problem had remained in abeyance, Koerber returned to it with the issue of his *Principles* on the subject (October 14, 1902) which differed little from what he had submitted to the Reconciliation Conference in 1900, and which was to be presented to a reestablished conference. The Czech reaction was quick and violent; the Young-Czech faction in the Parliament announced "the sharpest struggle against the Government [to be fought] with all the means customary in the Viennese Parliament."[49] For the time being, the threat was and was not carried out. True, in November, Koerber for the first time after the long pause was insulted by the Czech hecklers in the Parliament, but such obstruction as there was was a rather creeping one. The resuscitated "language conference" of 1902 lingered on until it proved a definite failure in January 1903.

The situation looked bleak; but all was not yet lost. Koerber contrived yet to achieve a distinct success when, after several months of tenacious negotiations with the Hungarians and with a great show of tension and drama, the compact with the Hungarians was finally achieved by a compromise on the last night of the year 1902. The threatened breach of Austro-Hungarian unity was thus avoided. The most complex documents of the compact, which included inter alia a complete customs tariff, were still to be submitted to the two parliaments, which in Austria Koerber did in January 1903. The Parliament obediently went into the First Reading in March 1903. The bill, however, was never reported back from the committees. Still, there was one more parliamentary success. The Parliament, in April 1903, adopted without obstruction the act concerning conscription of recruits, which, after new difficulties with Hungary, was passed again in final form in September 1903.

To what extent do these events bear on our main problem?

<hr/>

[49] Gustav Kolmer, *Parlament und Verfassung*, Vol. VIII, pp. 393-394.

They do inasmuch as they show that at that time it was still easier to threaten "sharpest struggle" against Koerber than to live up to the threat. For, despite the failure in the summer of 1902, the memory of the investment bills was still strong upon the minds and something like an inertia or rather a momentum from the preceding period still worked in favor of Koerber. There was uncertainty and dissent among the Czech parliamentarians, and the radicals in the faction insisting on obstruction were, it seems, in a minority. Kramář, the great leader of the Young-Czechs, was reported to have emphasized the difficult economic situation in Bohemia and expressed the opinion that in view of that he would advise postponing or adjourning the debates on the language question.[50] This was said as late as January 1903 as a private remark allegedly made in conversations in the Parliament. The correctness of the report is entirely on the conscience of the source mentioned in the previous footnote. But Kramář's remark is quite plausible, and as such it was, of course, "Koerberism" of pure water. Its coincidence with the Czech hesitations to push obstruction too far and the disunion among them does corroborate Kramář's point. Nevertheless, confusing time and space in an uneasy metaphor, one must say that Koerber's "plateau" had proved surprisingly long, but that in 1903 its end was being definitely reached, and a period of descent was ushered in. The Parliament was then again paralyzed by obstruction, and no legislative activity worth mentioning took place in the halls that were again disgraced by verbal crudities and at times by fist fights. Parliamentary passions were kept alive by all sorts of local riots and brawls, such as an attack of the Czech populace in Prague upon the German university students, riots by Slavic and German students in many places, excesses of the Germans in Innsbruck against the attempt to establish an Italian faculty there, the German opposition to the introduction of Polish language courses at teachers' colleges in Silesia, and other matters of similar earth-shaking significance. Thus, Koerber's word of a "parliamentary necropolis" was true merely in the deeper sense of the work that remained undone, because there was only too much noise in that cemetery.

[50] *Ibid.*, Vol. VIII, p. 445.

Four: Retrospect

Throughout all this, governing mostly with the help of the Emergency Article 14, Koerber remained true to his device of "passionless perseverance." He continued to work unbelievably hard, taking care of three ministries (Koerber had taken over the Ministry of Justice in October 1902), issuing a flood of long decrees. Among them was his decree to the governors, the chiefs of provincial administration, in which Koerber urged the rights of citizens concerned to inspect the (usually secret) files, as well as their right to be heard before decisions were made, inveighed against delays, and called for acceleration of bureaucratic processes. The decree contained an explicit reference to "the requirements of our time" (*Anforderungen der Jetztzeit*). This was in November 1903, but a year later, in November 1904, he still submitted to the Parliament a long memorandum concerning thorough-going modern reforms in public administration and a number of carefully prepared bills, dealing mostly with a series of economic bills on significant matters, but having no relation at all to any investment project. By that time, it should be added, Boehm-Bawerk had left the cabinet and Koerber had one Mansuet Kosel appointed in his stead. No evidence suggests, however, that at this late point Koerber felt that Boehm-Bawerk's departure had untied his hands. In fact, even earlier in the year, during a time when the Parliament was about to be prorogued, Koerber submitted to it a bill requiring approval of a loan of 159 million crowns to cover expenditures above the estimates in the construction of railroads under the Investment Act of 1901.[51] Apparently, no action on that bill ever occurred during Koerber's tenure of office. For the rest, undisturbed by the situation in the Parliament, Koerber continued his warnings and exhortations from the parliamentary tribune, urging his audience to struggle against economic misery, thus assuring for the population "laborious days and carefree nights." But the beautifully turned concluding passage of the speech was drowned in the turmoil of excitement over the riots in Prague.[52]

[51] *Stenographisches Protokoll, Haus der Abgeordneten*, Session XVII, Meeting 280 (May 10, 1904), Beilagen, Nr. 2036, contains a detailed description of all the unforeseeable technical difficulties in constructing the Tauern Railroad.

[52] *Stenographisches Protokoll, Haus der Abgeordneten*, Session XVII, Meeting 255 (March 8, 1904), p. 23356.

149

Four: Retrospect

Koerber's resignation is the complex and somewhat sordid story of an intrigue between Kramář and Minister of Foreign Affairs Goluchowski (who was settling the accounts of old disagreements) and perhaps of Koerber's successor, Gautsch. Sieghart's claim that the hostility of the "feudal" aristocracy against a "bourgeois" Prime Minister had something to do with Koerber's fall may have had some factual basis. It is true, however, that toward the end the various nationalities in the Parliament as well as the Catholics were opposed to Koerber. Things came to a head when the budget committee of the Parliament refused Koerber the approval of a loan of 15 million crowns for emergency needs and of 65 million for military expenditures. He took the refusal for a formal ground for resignation, pleading at the same time his own deteriorated health. It is claimed that the Emperor was glad to accept the resignation because Goluchowski had transmitted to the Emperor Kramář's promise to stop obstruction upon Koerber's demise. On the other hand, Baernreither's gossip coming from Frau Schratt claims that the Emperor never forgave Koerber's refusal to stay in office when the Emperor "with hands uplifted" had asked him to do so.[53] Whether this or that version is true and whether this or that individual factor was more or less responsible for the final outcome is of less interest within the context of this study than the plausibility of the statement that, given Koerber's different actions in the summer of 1902, his demise from premiership on December 31, 1904, after almost exactly a quinquennium of tenure would have been extremely improbable.[54]

[53] Joseph Maria Baernreither, *Fragments*, pp. 249-250.

[54] Only as an afterthought it may be added that there was an aftermath to Koerber's cabinet inasmuch as later (in 1905 and 1906) repeated attempts were made in the Parliament to submit Koerber, Boehm-Bawerk, Call, and Wittek (who had been in charge of the Railroad Ministry) to a procedure resembling impeachment because of over-expenditures in the construction of railroads and in the expansion of the Port of Triest. The inquiry came to nought, and the former ministers were completely exculpated. On the whole matter, see Alois Czedik, *Zur Geschichte*, Vol. II, pp. 349-352, 365. In pursuing this matter with considerable gusto, the parliamentarians were entirely oblivious of "the general enthusiasm with which the bill regarding the Alpine railroads had been passed by the House" (*ibid.*) and had to be explicitly reminded thereof by the inquiring commission in its report. This episode which so clearly revealed the change of mood and climate should be viewed as the parliamentary obituary to the Koerber plan and the Koerber era.

Four: Retrospect

At the very beginning of Koerber's career as Prime Minister, Herzl twice predicted for him "a long reign" and even repeated this prognosis almost three years later.[55] This prophecy, implying in contemporaneous Austrian terms that Koerber like Taaffe before him would remain in office for fourteen years, went awry. Koerber enjoyed political longevity as little as Herzl, who was dead by the time of Koerber's resignation, was allowed to enjoy physical longevity. Herzl had spoken as he did, because he understood the greatness and the novelty of Koerber's approach.[56] But Koerber's great spurt remained a failure and the Koerber era merely an episode. The only lasting effects were Koerber's innovations in the field of civil rights. None of Koerber's successors in the office dared touch the freedoms of press and assembly which Koerber had introduced, until the outbreak of the First World War brought about a period of unrestrained absolutism.

Yet Koerber's seminal idea, as has been shown, was hardly comprehended by contemporary and later writers, among whom Baron Czedik's understanding treatment is a lonely exception.[57] Intelligent observers, such as Kielmansegg and Joseph Redlich, did not hesitate to describe the man of the great idea as "a man of little devices" (*ein Mann der kleinen Mittel*).[58] By contrast, non-parliamentary and non-literary opinion remained friendly to Koerber. Without being too explicit about Koerber's basic idea but obviously showing traces of remembrance, the press and the voices of industry, banks, and commerce expressed great regrets at Koerber's departure, and for years ahead, whenever a change in premiership was in the offing, they invariably called for Koerber's return or described him as "the coming man."[59]

[55] Theodor Herzl, *Tagebuecher*, Vol. II, pp. 408, 414; Vol. III, p. 431.

[56] By contrast, Hantsch felt that Koerber's remaining in office "for full *four* years [a little error!] was a proof of Koerber's extra-ordinary ability." Cf. Hantsch, *Die Geschichte Oesterreichs*, Vol. II, p. 481.

[57] Cf. Alois Czedik, *Zur Geschichte*, Vol. II, e.g., pp. 314-315.

[58] Erich Graf Kielmansegg, *Kaiserhaus*, pp. 301 and 394; Joseph Redlich, *Schicksalsjahre*, Vol. II, p. 27.

[59] But Koerber continued for more than a decade (his activity in the Academy of Sciences apart) a perfectly private existence, until during the War he was first appointed Minister of Finance of Austria-Hungary and then became (in 1916) again the Prime Minister of Austria, from which post he was quickly dismissed by the Imperial successor to Francis Joseph, whom Koerber liked to call privately *der junge Herr*. It should be noted, however, that this study is not at all concerned with Koerber's biography, unless it has a bearing on the Koerber experiment.

Four: Retrospect

What remains to be discussed in the following pages is the twofold historical problem of the reason for Koerber's failure in 1902 and the lessons that emerged from his experiment. The former is of necessity conjectural or, if one likes, counterfactual. But it is cogitations of this kind that, despite their inherent uncertainty, are likely to cast light on, and promote our understanding of, very factual conditions and relationships. It is natural to look for an answer in Koerber's personality. Some people, including even a person who stood very close to Koerber, accused him of lack of energy (*Tatkraft*).[60]

But the accusation does not seem to hold water in view of the immense energy with which Koerber, even as the top civil servant in the Ministry of Commerce, gathered in his hands the guidance of all the departments of the Ministry. He did exactly the same during his premiership, making the heads of all the ministries (except Education and, alas and alack, Finance) into his subordinates, guiding their work and interfering with its details. For these reasons Koerber's office has been unsympathetically described as a "Super-Ministry" and the alleged decline in the responsibility of the individual ministries bemoaned without wasting praise on the increases in industry and efficiency that resulted from Koerber's prompting, proddings, and supervision.[61] It is because of this unrelenting activity that Redlich goes so far as to call Koerber a "thoroughly autocratic nature" and to speak of his "absolutist government"—charges that do not appear very sensible when leveled at a man who more than anyone else introduced elements of democracy into the worn texture of the Austrian *Obrigkeitsstaat*. Lack of energy was hardly characteristic of Koerber.

Closer to the mark may be the opinion of Sieghart, who, while fully recognizing Koerber's energy and courage,[62] speaks of Koerber's lack of an ability "to risk much in order to gain much."

Hence many occurrences and actions from the time of Koerber's lustrum have not been mentioned in the preceding pages.

[60] Baernreither, *Der Verfall*, p. 47; and Redlich, *Schicksalsjahre*, Vol. II, p. 17.

[61] Redlich, *Kaiser Franz Joseph*, p. 396; Baernreither, *Der Verfall*, p. 139.

[62] Victor Adler once (in 1902) doubted Koerber's courage. See *Aufsaetze, Reden, Briefe*, Vol. VIII, p. 230.

Koerber was not a gambler.[63] Sieghart also claims that Koerber had even hesitated to commit himself to the Canal Bill, because he shied away from "an adventurous financial policy."[64] The last phrase may possibly explain a great deal about Koerber's failure to approach the Reichsrat with a second large investment bill, the prerequisite for which would have been getting rid of Boehm-Bawerk and either taking over the Ministry of Finance himself or entrusting the job to someone devoted to him. Unless one assumes that Koerber was unable to rid himself of the ideas of financial orthodoxy he had imbibed as a young civil servant, his inaction at the crucial time is hard to understand. True, there was much talk about money being "squandered" by the investment policies. But as the ever-reasonable Czedik stresses, such talk had no foundation at all in facts.[65] Every action has its own uncertainties. But for Koerber to have acted in 1902 would have involved a minimum of "gambling."

Equally difficult to comprehend are Koerber's relations with Boehm-Bawerk. Koerber no doubt knew, must have known, if not from direct observation then from Minister of Commerce Call (whom Koerber did treat as a subordinate) of Boehm-Bawerk's persistent policy of obstruction and sabotage. It is true that Boehm-Bawerk's sharpest actions came very late in the game, and some of them may have remained secret. Nevertheless, Koerber was not in the habit to brook opposition with equanimity. By all accounts, he easily flared up and was given to violent fits of short temper, in the course of which he would throw bundles of files on the floor. And yet, there is no evidence at all of any displeasure with Boehm-Bawerk, let alone of animosity toward him. In fact, in the years following the demise of Koerber's cabinet, he and Boehm-Bawerk appear to have remained on best social terms, would meet frequently, and would dine and wine each other.[66]

[63] Rudolf Sieghart, *Die letzten Jahrzehnte einer Grossmacht*, p. 49.

[64] *Ibid.*, p. 58.

[65] Alois Czedik, *Zur Geschichte*, p. 318. In our own time it was left to the superficiality of Koerber's modern biographer to mention with satisfaction the millions which the Austrian state had saved by *not* building the canals. Cf. Herwig Leitgeb, "Die Ministerpraesidentshaft Dr. Ernest von Koerbers," p. 53.

[66] See Redlich, *Schicksalsjahre*, Vol. 1, pp. 34, 78, 79.

The whole relationship is rather enigmatic. But then Koerber *was* an enigmatic person, as has been noted by a perceptive civil servant who had worked under him.[67]

Nor is it clear why the Canal Bill of 1901 was technically less well prepared than Koerber's bills usually were. Why did the usually prompting and prodding Koerber allow the experts at the Ministry of Commerce to take such a long time ironing out the technological problems of the canal construction, thus giving the Ministry of Finance many pretexts for continuing their tactics of procrastination? Despite Sieghart's assertions of his interest in the Canal Bill, one misses in the *Motivation* attached to the bill the hand of Sieghart who took particular pride in preparing the bills far in advance. In this connection, one must add that Sieghart apparently left Koerber in the lurch in the summer of 1902. At any rate, there is no evidence that the far-sighted Sieghart urged his chief to save his great experiment by injecting new life and investing additional millions into it. Sieghart's passivity at that time casts light on the previously treated question (*vide* Lecture Two) as to who was the main moving agent behind the Koerber plan, and it tends to corroborate the view that it was Koerber's *ingenium* that stood behind the plan. It was only years later, after much water had run down the Danube, and none through the canals, that Sieghart, then working under Prime Minister Beck, suddenly started pondering the "popular idea" of returning to a large investment project—a policy which he regarded as quite "feasible." Sieghart expressed these thoughts in a private letter to Beck.[68] This sounded very much like a pupil's recollection of his old teacher's instruction.

Much has been said in the preceding lectures about the manifold tasks that deflected Koerber from his main pursuit. But in that summer of 1902 there were other things that claimed Koerber's attention. I am, of course, not referring to a resumption of the Czech-German language conferences because a new investment project would have again deprived the language problem of importance and actuality. But it was precisely in that summer

[67] The reference is to the previously quoted Robert Ehrhart, *Im Dienst des alten Oesterreich*, p. 360.

[68] Cf. Alfred Ableitinger, "Rudolf Sieghart," p. 253. Letter of April 1, 1907.

of 1902 that the compact with Hungary began to loom large on the horizon and to place enormous claims on Koerber's time and energy. Just as the Koerber experiment involved the problem of the creation of an economically more unified and more meaningful territory of Cisleithania, the negotiations with Hungary also turned around the maintenance of the economic unity of the Monarchy as a whole.

Finally, one more remark is needed on a previously treated subject. Naumann was quoted as having said with regard to Austria of the early years of the century: "What is needed here is a Napoleon; not necessarily Napoleon I, also Napoleon III would do."[69] Koerber did not possess the dictatorial power of either Napoleon. But, power apart, what separated him from Napoleon III was the lack of a broad ideology of industrialization or economic development with which the Saint-Simonians had equipped their Emperor. This has been discussed before. But what should be added here is the conjecture that if Koerber had had such an ideology at his disposal, he very likely would have been its intellectual captive and would have found it very difficult to resist the ideological pressure for action in the fateful summer of 1902.

The Koerber experiment ended in failure, and thus it is the task of the historian to discuss the failure and to try to explain its causes. But at the same time, he must not overlook the great success that stood beside and behind the failure. In that success lies the important historical lesson that emerged from the experiment. The success was little short of amazing. A country that for years had been torn asunder by a strife that appeared irreconcilable and suffering from a malady that appeared incurable and, to many observers, terminal was suddenly united by the appeal, by word and deed, to the economic interests of the population. Suddenly, the Germans and the Czechs who had been separated by seemingly

---

[69] Cf. Otto Bauer, *Die Nationalitaetenfrage und die Sozialdemokratie*, Vienna, 1907, p. 430. It is both curious and illuminating that in his remarkable book Bauer, one of the very few eminent representatives of Marxist thought after Marx, hardly pays any attention to the Koerber experiment. The reason must lie in the fact that in Bauer's mind the national revolutions had acquired a paramount importance, and it was to them that he tried to apply the concepts of Marxian analysis. We shall return to this point presently.

unbridgeable hatreds by one fell blow discovered their common interests.[70]

It is true that many voices in literature were raised to deplore that those who followed Koerber's leadership were moved by egotism rather than concern for the welfare of the State. This high-sounding idealism, whose prophets would like to excise the basic category of interest from political science and sociology, cannot be taken too seriously. No historian worth his salt should fail to see that the alleged contrast was nothing but a hollow sham, because nothing strengthened the Austrian state so much as the successful appeal to "egotism."

It is tempting to speculate whether a continuation of the Koerber experiment on an expanded and expanding scale might have increased the cohesion of the country and thus changed a great deal in the course of the decade that followed the Koerber regime. But the temptation must be resisted, and this not just to avoid stepping into the morass of the unknowables. Once one begins to think in very broad terms, the terrible geographic limitations of the Koerber experiment leap to mind. For Croatia, and with it most of the Yugoslav national protest, was firmly held in the grip of the Hungarian nobility so that the dualism of the Monarchy served as an insurmountable barrier to the best conceived economic policies originating in Vienna.

And the lesson of history? It speaks with a voice that is both clear and strong and can be summarized in a single phrase: The primacy of the economic factor.[71] It is quite possible that the validity of this lesson transcends the spatial and temporal limits of

---

[70] In fact, as Karl Kraus, who disliked Koerber, put it in a malicious but correct comment, the canal project united those Germans and the Czechs who welcomed the canals as well as those Germans and the Czechs who opposed them. See *Die Fackel*, Vol. III: 78 (End of May 1901). The comment referred to the period of parliamentary negotiations over the Canal Bill, but remained applicable also to the subsequent periods, except that the friends of the canals among the population constituted an overwhelming majority.

[71] Otto Bauer's rather surprising neglect of the Koerber experiment may be explicable by Bauer's intellectual difficulty. The practice of Koerber's economic policies (unwittingly, of course) offered strong support to the basic tenets of traditional Marxism, while Bauer's innovating stress on national revolution pointed in a very different direction.

the subject matter dealt with in the present study. How far it does so may well be the subject of another research project. At any rate, in a country and in a period where and when even the international ideology of the Social Democratic labor movement proved unable to withstand the impact of the nationality strife that threatened to split the party and the labor unions, Koerber demonstrated that economic interests, intelligently and imaginatively appealed to, could be stronger than the reputedly invincible nationalist aspirations.

To repeat and to conclude: With intelligence and imagination Koerber had tried great things. For various reasons, good and bad, he did not finish the job. But his failure must not forfeit his claim to our respect and admiration. In the wise words of the great Stoic which have been chosen as a motto for these lectures: *Egerunt, sed non peregerunt, suspiciendi tamen sunt.*

Jahrgang 1901.

Reichsgesetzblatt

für die

im Reichsrathe vertretenen Königreiche und Länder.

XXX. Stück. — Ausgegeben und versendet am 13. Juni 1901.

Inhalt: № 66. Gesetz, betreffend den Bau von Wasserstraßen und die Durchführung von Flußregulirungen

66.

Gesetz vom 11. Juni 1901.

betreffend den Bau von Wasserstraßen und die Durchführung von Flußregulirungen.

Mit Zustimmung beider Häuser des Reichsrathes finde Ich anzuordnen, wie folgt:

§. 1.

Der Bau von Wasserstraßen, und zwar:

a) eines Schiffartscanales von der Donau zur Oder,

b) eines Schiffahrtscanales von der Donau zur Moldau nächst Budweis nebst der Canalisirung der Moldau von Budweis bis Prag,

c) eines Schiffahrtscanales vom Donau-Odercanal zur mittleren Elbe nebst Canalisirung der Elbe strecke von Melnik bis Jaromer,

d) einer schiffbaren Verbindung vom Donau-Oder canal zum Stromgebiete der Weichsel und bis zu einer schiffbaren Strecke des Dniester

ist vom Staate auszuführen, wenn das Land, in dem einer der unter a bis d genannten Canäle oder Canal theile hergestellt werden soll, beziehungsweise eine der oben angeführten zu canalisirenden Flußstrecken sich befindet, sich verpflichtet die Zahlung eines jährlichen Betrages zu leisten, der zur Verzinsung und Amorti sirung eines Achtels jener Obligationen hinreicht, welche zur Herstellung des betreffenden Canales oder Canaltheiles, beziehungsweise zur Canalisirung der betreffenden Flußstrecke (a bis d) emittirt werden.

Zu diesem Zwecke ist das Land berechtigt, die Interessenten heranzuziehen.

Die Beiträge der Länder sind nach Maßgabe der den Staat aus diesem Anlasse treffenden Zahlungen zu leisten und haben aufzuhören, wenn die Einnahmen des betreffenden Canales nach Abzug der Erhaltungs und Betriebskosten den zur Verzinsung und Amorti sirung des Nominalanlagecapitales dieses Canales erforderlichen Betrag durch zwei aneinander folgende Jahre überschritten haben.

§. 2.

Die Vorsorge für Beiträge aus Landesmitteln, sowie die Art der Heranziehung der innerhalb der einzelnen Königreiche und Länder in Betracht kommenden Interessenten bleibt der Landesgesetzgebung vorbehalten.

Der Landesbeitrag kann, falls eine diesbezügliche Vereinbarung zwischen der Staatsverwaltung und dem betreffenden Lande zustande kommt, auch durch die Herstellung einzelner in den Bauprojecten vor gesehenen Anlagen (Häfen, Anlandeplätze, Zufahrts straßen u. s. w.), durch die Abtretung von Grund eigenthum, Einräumung von dinglichen Rechten und Überlassung von Wasserrechten, Materiallieferungen, sowie sonstige Sach- und Arbeitsleistungen abgestattet werden.

§. 3.

Für die einheitliche Leitung der im §. 1 näher bezeichneten Arbeiten ist in entsprechender Weise Vor sorge zu treffen.

Es ist ein aus Fachmännern und Vertretern der Interessenten bestehender Beirath zu bestellen. Die Hälfte der Mitglieder des Beirathes ist von der Re

159

gierung, die andere Hälfte von den Landesausschüssen der betheiligten Länder zu ernennen.

Die näheren Bestimmungen über Zahl und Vertheilung der Mitglieder und die Geschäftsführung sind im Verordnungswege zu erlassen. Bei der Zusammensetzung dieses Beirathes ist auf die Interessen des Handels, der Industrie, des Gewerbes, der Land- und Forstwirtschaft, sowie der Arbeiterschaft Rücksicht zu nehmen.

§. 4.

Die Verwaltung der nach §. 1 dieses Gesetzes herzustellenden Wasserstraßen, sowie die Festsetzung und Einhebung der Abgaben und Gebüren für die Benützung der Wasserstraßen und der dazu gehörigen Anlagen erfolgt durch den Staat.

Bei Feststellung dieser Abgaben und Gebüren ist auf den ausgiebigsten Schutz der gesammten heimischen Production, insbesondere durch entsprechende tarifarische Maßregeln, vollste Rücksicht zu nehmen.

§. 5.

Behufs Sicherstellung der Regulirung derjenigen Flüsse in Böhmen, Mähren, Schlesien, Galizien, Nieder- und Oberösterreich, welche mit den im §. 1 genannten Canälen, canalisirten und in Canalisirung begriffenen Flüssen ein einheitliches Gewässernetz bilden und es, sei es wegen der Zufuhr von Wasser, sei es mit Rücksicht auf die Geschiebebewegung für die in Betracht kommenden Wasserstraßen besondere Bedeutung besitzen, sind die Verhandlungen mit den betheiligten Königreichen und Ländern sofort einzuleiten, wobei für die finanziellen Leistungen der Königreiche und Länder die bei solchen Maßnahmen bisher üblichen Gesichtspunkte Anwendung zu finden haben. Die Regulirung dieser Flüsse muß spätestens gleichzeitig mit dem Bau der Canäle (§. 6, Absatz 1) in Angriff genommen werden.

Für alle übrigen Wasserläufe in den im Reichsrathe vertretenen Königreichen und Ländern, hinsichtlich welcher sich eine Regulirung als nothwendig darstellt, ist dieselbe thunlichst rasch vorzubereiten und sobald die entsprechenden Vorarbeiten vorliegen, ehestens in Angriff zu nehmen.

Die behufs Durchführung solcher Regulirungen erforderliche Erhöhung des jährlichen Staatsvertrages für den Meliorationsfond ist durch ein besonderes Gesetz festzustellen.

Die Einstellung von Dotationen für Wasserbauten in die jeweiligen Staatsvoranschläge bleibt hiedurch unberührt.

§. 6.

Der Bau der im §. 1 bezeichneten Wasserstraßen, hinsichtlich welcher seitens der Vertretungen der betreffenden Länder zustimmende Beschlüsse im Sinne des §. 1 gefaßt worden sind, hat längstens im Jahre 1904 zu beginnen.

Die erforderlichen Vorarbeiten sind derart rechtzeitig durchzuführen, daß dieser Zeitpunkt eingehalten und der Bau längstens binnen 20 Jahren vollendet werden kann.

§. 7.

Beim Bau der Canäle und der Canalisirung der Flüsse sind, soweit dies mit dem gedeihlichen Fortgang der Arbeit vereinbar ist, inländische Techniker und Arbeiter sowie die heimische Industrie zu beschäftigen.

§. 8.

Die Kosten der Herstellung der in §. 1 bezeichneten Wasserstraßen und der nach §. 5, Absatz 1, durchzuführenden Flußregulirungen sind erforderlichenfalls, soweit diese Kosten nicht durch die Leistungen der Länder oder sonstiger Interessenten, beziehungsweise aus dem Meliorationsfonde gedeckt wurden, durch eine mit höchstens 4 Procent steuerfrei zu verzinsende, auf Kronenwährung lautende, in 90 Jahren zu tilgende Anleihe zu beschaffen.

Die Regierung wird ermächtigt, von dieser Anleihe in der Bauperiode 1904 bis Ende 1912 einen Maximalbetrag von 250 Millionen Kronen Nominale auszugeben. Der hieraus erzielte Erlös darf nur zur Deckung der Herstellungskosten der im §. 1 bezeichneten Wasserstraßen und der im §. 5, Absatz 1, vorgesehenen Regulirungen verwendet werden.

Von dem Anlehenserlöse ist ein Betrag im Höchstausmaße von 75,000.000 K für die erwähnten Regulirungen zu widmen.

Die Regierung hat alljährlich zugleich mit der Einbringung des Staatsvoranschlages einen Ausweis vorzulegen, aus welchem die Beträge der auf Rechnung der erwähnten 250 Millionen Kronen Nominale ausgegebenen Obligationen, sowie die Verwendung des Erlöses derselben während der letztabgelaufenen Rechnungsperiode und die in dieser Zeit stattgehabten Arbeiten genau zu ersehen sind.

§. 9.

Die Deckung des nach dem Jahre 1912 sich ergebenden Erfordernisses ist rechtzeitig durch ein besonderes Gesetz sicherzustellen.

§. 10

Die Regierung wird ermächtigt, die Trace und die technische Anlage der im §. 1 erwähnten Wasserstraßen nach Einvernahme der Landesausschüsse der betreffenden Länder endgiltig festzusetzen.

Appendix I

Jede Abweichung von dem nach den Bestimmungen des §. 1 aufgestellten Programme der herzustellenden Wasserstraßen und jede Erweiterung des Programmes über den Rahmen des §. 1 hinaus bedarf einer besonderen gesetzlichen Bewilligung.

§. 11.

Für die Deckung der aus der Begebung der Anleihe erwachsenden Annuitätslast hat der Finanzminister vor dem Baubeginne (§. 6) gegebenenfalls Vorschläge zur verfassungsmäßigen Behandlung zu unterbreiten.

§. 12.

Die für die Vorarbeiten (§. 6, Alinea 2) erforderlichen Beträge sind alljährlich im Staatsvoranschlage anzusprechen.

§. 13.

Für die im §. 1 und §. 5, Absatz 1, bezeichneten Anlagen steht das Enteignungsrecht, insbesondere auch das Recht auf gänzliche oder theilweise Entziehung von Privatgewässern und Wasserrechten zu, wobei für die Durchführung der Enteignung die Bestimmungen des Gesetzes vom 18. Februar 1878, R. G. Bl. Nr. 30, betreffend die Enteignung zum Zwecke der Herstellung und des Betriebes von Eisenbahnen, sinngemäße Anwendung zu finden haben.

Bei der Aufstellung und Ausführung der Projecte ist nach Thunlichkeit auf die Interessen der Wasserwirtschaft und insbesondere darauf Rücksicht zu nehmen, daß der Bedarf an Trinkwasser, sowie an dem zum Wirtschaftsbetriebe und für die Fälle der Feuersgefahr nöthigen Wasser für die Gemeinden, Ortschaften und Ansiedlungen gedeckt bleibe.

Bei der Feststellung der Projecte, sowie beim Betriebe der künstlichen Wasserstraßen ist insbesondere auch auf die bestehenden landwirtschaftlichen Meliorationen, so namentlich auf die Bewässerungen und Entwässerungen thunliche Rücksicht zu nehmen, wobei jedoch auch nach Möglichkeit dahin zu wirken ist, daß in Verbindung mit den neuen Wasserstraßen solche den landwirtschaftlichen Betrieb fördernde Anlagen neu hergestellt werden können. Hiebei sind in erster Linie die Interessen des bäuerlichen Grundbesitzes zu berücksichtigen.

Alle Angelegenheiten, welche sich auf die Feststellung und Ausführung der Projecte für die im §. 1 bezeichneten Anlagen beziehen, sowie die darauf bezüglichen Entscheidungen fallen in die Competenz des zur Baudurchführung berufenen Handelsministeriums, welches mit den anderen betheiligten Ministerien das Einvernehmen zu pflegen hat.

Die näheren Bestimmungen werden im Verordnungswege erlassen werden.

§. 14.

Sobald eine der im §. 1 und §. 5, Absatz 1, angeführten Bauten in Angriff genommen wird, ernennt der Handelsminister im Einvernehmen mit dem Minister des Innern die erforderliche Anzahl von Gewerbeinspectoren, deren Thätigkeit im Sinne des Gesetzes vom 17. Juni 1883, R. G. Bl. Nr. 117, sich auf die Überwachung der betreffenden Bau-, Erd- und Wasserbauarbeiten erstreckt. Auf diese Gewerbeinspectoren finden alle Bestimmungen des bezeichneten Gesetzes Anwendung. Sie sind Mitglieder des Beirathes (§. 3). Nach Bedarf sind ihnen die nöthigen Hilfsorgane an die Seite zu stellen. Diese Gewerbeinspectoren sind insbesondere verpflichtet, von ihnen alljährlich zu erstattenden Berichten genaue Angaben über die Lohn-, Wohnungs- und Sanitätsverhältnisse der bei der Ausführung der bezeichneten Bauten beschäftigten Arbeitspersonen, sowie über die Art der Arbeitsvergebung und über die Arbeitszeit zusammenzustellen.

Die durch die Bestellung und Amtsführung dieser Gewerbeinspectoren hervorgerufenen Kosten fallen zu Lasten der Baufonde.

Zur Überwachung des sanitären Zustandes unter den bei der Ausführung der bezeichneten Bauten beschäftigten Arbeitspersonen sind nach Bedarf besondere ärztliche Organe zu bestellen.

§. 15.

Sämmtliche Bestimmungen des VI. Hauptstückes der Gewerbeordnung, einschließlich der Bestimmungen der §§. 88a, 96a, 96b finden auf alle Kategorien von Arbeitern Anwendung, welche bei der Ausführung einer der im §. 1 und §. 5, Absatz 1 angeführten Bauten beschäftigt sind.

§. 16.

Verträge, bücherliche Eintragungen, Eingaben und sonstige Urkunden, durch welche zum Zwecke der Sicherstellung der im §. 1 dieses Gesetzes bezeichneten Anlagen die Erwerbung von Grund und Boden, die Einräumung dinglicher Rechte, die Überlassung von Wasserrechten, die Beistellung von Bau- und Betriebsmaterialien, die Leistung von Vorzahlungen oder sonstigen, wie immer gearteten Beiträgen zugesichert oder Vereinbarungen zum Zwecke der Capitalsbeschaffung und des Baues der bezeichneten Anlagen getroffen werden, mit Ausschluß der im gerichtlichen Verfahren in Streitsachen stattfindenden Verhandlungen, endlich die von den Ländern, den Bezirken und Gemeinden zur Beschaffung des für die Zwecke der

Beitragsleistung zu den Kosten der Wasserstraße (§. 1) nothwendigen Capitales etwa aufzunehmenden Anleihen genießen die Stempel- und Gebührenfreiheit.

Dieselbe Begünstigung genießen die von den Interessenten etwa zu überreichenden Eingaben, Plane und sonstigen Schriftstücke, durch welche die Ausführung dieser Anlagen in technischer oder finanzieller Beziehung vorbereitet wird.

Die im §. 11 des Gesetzes vom 30. Juni 1884, R. G. Bl. Nr. 116, enthaltenen Begünstigungen für Meliorationsunternehmungen finden auch auf die im § 5, Absatz 1, erwähnten Regulirungen Anwendung.

§. 17.

Mit dem Vollzuge dieses Gesetzes ist Mein Gesammtministerium beauftragt.

Wien, am 11. Juni 1901.

Franz Joseph m. p

Koerber m. p.	**Welsersheimb** m. p
Wittek m. p.	**Böhm** m. p.
Spens m. p.	**Hartel** m. p.
Rezek m. p.	**Call** m. p.
Giovanelli m. p.	**Piętak** m. p.

The Original Text of Boehm-Bawerk's Secret Draft for an Amendment of the Canal Act of June 11, 1901.

GESETZ

vom . . . .

womit das Gesetz vom 11. Juni 1901, R.G.Bl. Nr. 66 betreffend den Bau von Wasserstrassen und die Durchfuehrung von Flussregulierungen abgeaendert wird.

Mit Zustimmung beider Haeuser des Reichsrates finde Ich anzuordnen wie folgt:

Art. I.

Der im Paragraph 6 des Gesetzes vom 11. Juni 1901, R.G.Bl. Nr. 66 betreffend den Bau von Wasserstrassen und die Durchfuehrung von Flussregulierungen vorgesehene Termin, in welchem mit dem Baue der im Paragraph 1 dieses Gesetzes bezeichneten Wasserstrassen laengstens zu beginnen ist, wird bis zum Jahre 1907 erstreckt.

Dagegen sind die im Paragraph 5, Abs. 1 vorgesehenen Flussregulierungen, entsprechend dem aus Paragraph 3, Abs. 1 im Zusammenhalte mit Paragraph 6, Abs. 1 des bezeichneten Gesetzes sich ergebenden Termine, im Jahre 1904 in Angriff zu nehmen.

Desgleichen hat die Vollendung des Baues der im Paragraph 1 des Gesetzes vom 11. Juni, R.G.Bl. Nr. 66 bezeichneten Wasserstrassen im Sinne der bisherigen Bestimmung des Paragraph 6 Abs. 2, dieses Gesetzes laengstens im Jahre 1923 zu erfolgen.

Art. II.

Mit dem Vollzuge dieses Gesetzes, welches mit dem Tage seiner Kundmachung in Wirksamkeit tritt, ist Mein Gesamtministerium beauftragt.

BEGRUENDUNG.

Abgesehen von den Schwierigkeiten technischer und administrativer Natur, welche sich der Inangriffnahme des Baues der Wasserstrassen noch im laufenden Jahre entgegenstellen, wuerde es auch die momentane finanzielle Lage des Staates nicht gestatten, an die Durchfuehrung des Kanalbauten Programmes zu schreiten, ohne dass fuer die aus der Begebung der bezueglichen Anleihe erwachsende Annuitaetenlast eine spezielle Deckung geschaffen wuerde.

Obwohl Paragraph 11 des Wasserstrassengesetzes bereits eine diesbezuegliche Ermaechtigung enthaelt, haelt die Regierung mit Ruecksicht auf die ganze wirtschaftliche Lage den gegenwaertigen Zeitpunkt fuer durchaus ungeeignet, um mit einem derartigen Vorschlage hervorzutreten.

Um einerseits diesem Gesichtspunkte, andrerseits der Lage der Staatsfinanzen Rechnung zu tragen, sieht die Regierung ein entsprechendes Auskunftsmittel in der Verschiebung des Baubeginnes der Wasserstrassen, von welcher Massregel jedoch die vielfach dringlicheren, teilweise auch schon in Angriff genommenen Flussregulierungsarbeiten ausgenommen sein sollen.

Von massgebender Bedeutung fuer die Entschliessung der Regierung ist auch die Erwaegung, dass in den zunaechst kommenden Jahren der gegenwaertig ohnehin nicht sehr aufnahmsfaehige Markt durch Kreditoperationen zum Zwecke der Beschaffung der Geldmittel fuer ganz unaufschiebbare Zwecke soweit in Anspruch genommen werden muss, dass an die Emission eines bedeutenderen Teiles der Wasserstrassenanleihe nicht gut gedacht werden kann.

Nachdem durch die Massregel, wie der Gesetzentwurf ausdruecklich betont, eine Hinausschiebung des Vollendungstermines der Kanalbauten nicht bewirkt werden soll, so bedeutet die ganze Aktion lediglich eine Verkuerzung der Bauzeit und wird daher ein rascheres Tempo in den Bauarbeiten im Gefolge haben, was im Interesse einer oekonomischen Baufuehrung nur erwuenscht sein kann.

INDEX OF PROPER NAMES

Index of Proper Names

Library of Congress Cataloging in Publication Data

Gerschenkron, Alexander.
    An economic spurt that failed.

    (Janeway lectures, Princeton University)
    Includes index.
    1.   Austria—Economic policy—Addresses, essays, lec-
tures.   2.   Austrian school of economists—Addresses,
essays, lectures.   I.   Title.   II.   Series: The Eliot
Janeway lectures on historical economics in honor of
Joseph Schumpeter; [1973]
HC265.G44   330.9′436′04   76-45898
ISBN 0-691-04216-0

Milton Keynes UK
Ingram Content Group UK Ltd.
UKHW020720101124
450942UK00006B/291